Animals Have
More Sense

Animals Have More Sense

Sid Jenkins

Edited by Michael Leitch

COLLINS

──────────────To Sue ──────────

William Collins Sons & Co. Ltd
London · Glasgow · Sydney
Auckland · Toronto · Johannesburg

First published in 1987
© Sid Jenkins 1987

British Library Cataloguing in Publication Data

Jenkins, Sid
Animals have more sense.
1. Animals, Treatment of
I. Title
179'.3'0924   HV4708

ISBN 0 00 412281X

Printed in Great Britain by
Robert Hartnoll (1985) Ltd

CONTENTS

— THE LEARNING YEARS —

Always there was Punch and Judy. As far back as I can remember we had Punch the cat, and Judy the dog who came to us when I was aged one.

They were my friends and companions during the Second World War. While the bombs dropped on Swansea, I sat under the table and stroked the cat. I can remember doing it; it must have helped to reassure a small boy who did not know what was going on.

The German air force struck many heavy blows at ports like Swansea; but I did not know that. I saw pretty lights above the city, and that is what they were to me, not shell-bursts or bombs or tracer bullets.

We had an Anderson shelter in the garden, but my grandmother was severely disabled and bedridden, and as no one wanted to leave her by herself we mostly stayed indoors. I had a tent under the table, and Punch and Judy sat with me. Sometimes they sat on top of me, so I was kept warm as well as comforted.

Every so often Judy came into season and went out roaming in the streets. She never seemed to lack for mates and in due course a new litter of puppies arrived. These were disposed of in the way that was then customary: they were put in a bucket of water and a lid was placed on top.

For a short time the drowning puppies made a pathetic squeaking noise inside the bucket. 'What are they doing?' I asked, and was always told: 'They're singing.'

I thought of questioning this no more than I thought of questioning the practice of making puppies somehow disappear by putting them in a bucket (I came to know that I never saw them again afterwards). Several years were to pass before I understood what had happened, and a few years more before I understood that I disapproved of it, and could explain why.

The end of the war gave me little cause for satisfaction. We moved from our comfortable house in Swansea, which had a garden and a bathroom, into a back-to-back in Leeds which had neither. It was a grim place, compared with what I had known; cramped and alien. Worst of all, we could not bring the animals with us. In Swansea I had to say goodbye to Punch and Judy, my companions and protectors since the beginning of time.

I was probably more upset at losing Punch and Judy than I was on seeing my future home and its gloomy surroundings, but the two events combined to fill me with misery. My refuge, where I could escape from the new house, was a farm. By one of those rare strokes of good fortune, out of all the countless rows of back-to-backs in Leeds in which I might have found myself, our street ended next to a farm.

It was an unlikely place for a farm to be. All along the bottom end of it were mills and foundries; in one place they made coal-bricks. Somehow the farm had stood its ground during and after the industrial invasion, and in the 1940s there it was still. The farm buildings remain to this day.

To me it was a godsend: open space, fields where I could go and wander. The farmers, two brothers called Warrington to whom I shall be forever grateful, did not mind if this particular small grimy neighbour wanted to visit their land and look around. Very soon I was helping – to pick mangels or turnips, I remember, and to work with the animals, bringing the cows up to the yard.

There was nowhere much to go wrong, no roads to cross; I watched the farmers call their cattle and copied what they did. The cows knew where to go anyway. A leader went to the head of the file and then the others sorted themselves out in their pecking order and off they went.

As I grew older I was allowed to go down to another field, further away, and fetch the cows in from there. All the time I was learning about animals. I learned soon enough that cows could kick, and that they could kick out sideways as well as backwards. In those days of hand-milking, to place cold hands on their teats could well provoke a hoof to fly out and catch you. With cows, I learned, you had to be wary within a large radius of the animal's backside. This was different from horses, who generally struck out in a backwards-only direction.

I already had some experience of horses, or rather, a horse. It was a fat old thing that used to pull the coalman's cart in Aberaman, near Aberdare, where I had gone occasionally to stay with an adopted aunt and uncle; he was a signalman on the railway. One of my treats was being allowed to sit up with the coalman on his delivery rounds.

The horse was docile enough when harnessed to the cart. After working hours, when he was turned out into a field, he was more unpredictable. I went into the field to see him one day. I was stroking his hindquarters; next thing I was on my back, seeing stars. My uncle had witnessed this from his signalbox, which he left in a hurry to try to protect me from further blows and carry me home.

Although, going back to our street in Leeds, everyone lived in a little brick box tightly packed against the neighbours, people had more contact with farm animals than you would find in a similar street today. Our street has since been pulled down, so I cannot make a direct comparison, but I do remember that there were piggeries nearby, and people had allotments on which they kept chickens. A third Warrington brother had a house near us and he kept chickens at the top end, in a place known to all as 'Up Yonder'. Coming from Wales, I hadn't a clue what it meant, but if I saw him heading in that direction I would run across and ask:

'Are you going Up Yonder, Mr Warrington?'

'Yes, come on if you want to come.'

I would go up there with him, while he carried his bucket of swill and whatever else he had saved for feeding his chickens. I liked standing around and watching those chickens, and today I know why. They were free. They went about where they wanted, laying eggs wherever it suited them and eating when they chose. So different from today's factory methods – the automatic cages and the prison atmosphere. I remember thinking back to the chickens from Up Yonder when recently I had to investigate a very badly neglected battery unit (this was one of the episodes filmed for the TV series *Animal Squad*, see page 20).

What a difference. At the battery unit, dead hens were everywhere, piled up on top of each other in rusty cages where they had lived their brief and cruelly constricted lives. Today, to keep within the law, a chicken farmer need only provide a living space per bird as large as a sheet of foolscap paper. That is all. In my childhood it was normal for the hens to go where they pleased, either in a yard or a specially constructed run. If they wanted to lay their eggs in the nestboxes, they did so; if not, they laid them on the floor and the owner had to find them. I am glad, when I go out on cases today, that I have that standard of comparison. It may not be available to future generations.

After some years in the back-to-back we moved to a house on one of the estates, which had – oh, luxury – its own bathroom. I tried to maintain my contact with animals through my school years, though it was not always easy. I left school and in due course joined the Army. Here, again, an episode presented itself which made me think hard about animals and the way we treat them.

I was in a camp near Nienburg in West Germany. A dog had been wandering loose about the camp for several days. Eventually, because it might have rabies, an order was given for the dog to be destroyed.

I was on duty the day it was done. The dog was brought out on a rope and held while a hole was dug next to the place where it stood. I remember looking at the dog while its grave was being prepared, and thinking how pitiful and frightened it was.

When the hole was ready, the Regimental Sergeant-Major took a .303 rifle, walked towards the dog, raised the rifle and fired. As he pulled the trigger, the dog moved to one side and the first shot failed to kill it. A sergeant took over the rifle from the RSM. Another round was loaded and fired, and this one killed the dog.

I felt a lot of resentment about the way every aspect of the task had been handled. I knew there must be a better, more humane method and I voiced some of my feelings to the RSM. He, no doubt, was upset at having failed to shoot the dog properly, and I was promptly told in typical Army fashion to shut my mouth and keep it shut.

It was another episode, and I mentally filed away what I had seen and what I had learned from it. Instead of simply feeling sorry for the dog, I progressed some way towards the idea that even when an animal faced death, it should be respected and treated humanely. Also, I saw, the destruction of an animal needed to be done properly, by someone trained to carry out the task in the most humane way possible.

I was still some years away from joining the RSPCA, but already I had begun to think along similar lines. It was not until nine years after the incident in the Army camp that I at last found myself setting out with twenty-seven other trainee inspectors on the RSPCA's course at their headquarters in Horsham, Sussex. Then for the first time I got to grips with the professional approach to animal care, studying a whole range of subjects including law, animal husbandry, rescue techniques and humane destruction.

I was on my way to the kind of career that I had always wanted, even though I had never quite realized this before. By the time I finished the course I had been to agricultural college, learned how to look after horses at Knightsbridge Barracks in London and the British Equestrian Centre at Stoneleigh, and done much else besides. I had even trained as a slaughterman in a slaughterhouse.

This was an especially tough part of the course, and several of the trainees could not bring themselves to go through with it. I too had my doubts, and even wondered if we were not acting in opposition to the ideals of the Society by learning how to kill animals instead of concentrating on how to preserve and care for them. Later, when I was qualified and putting what I had learned into practice, I soon understood.

Suppose a slaughterman is not doing his job properly. How can he be put right if the RSPCA officer cannot show him what he is doing wrong? It happened to me, and I was able to rise to the occasion – thanks to my training. Again, suppose a horse is badly injured by the roadside, and must be swiftly and humanely destroyed. It is far better if a vet or RSPCA man is on hand to do the job in the proper manner than to leave the animal to suffer, or entrust its destruction to some passing farmer who happens to have a gun.

Those were some of the things I learned in my early years with the RSPCA, which I joined in 1973. My first posting as an inspector was to a station in West Wales. Later I returned to Yorkshire as inspector for Harrogate, and now I am responsible for a group covering mainly the western part of the county. Our headquarters are in Leeds, and we have inspectors based in Leeds, Bradford, Halifax, Huddersfield, Skipton and Harrogate. Most of the events related in this book took place in one or other of those two very different parts of the country: Wales and Yorkshire. For what they reveal about animals, and our attitudes towards them, they could have happened anywhere in Britain.

—— JENKINS THE GOOSE ——

When I was posted to West Wales as an RSPCA inspector, I was new to the job as well as to the region. Although I too was Welsh, I was not from *that* part of Wales, and I prepared myself for at least one special 'welcome in the hillside', whatever form it might take.

I did not have to wait long. Barely, or so it seemed, had I fallen asleep on my first night in my new house when I was woken by the sound of the telephone. I picked it off the hook and before I had a chance to mutter into the receiver, a voice cried:

'Is that you, boyo?'

'Yes,' I replied, my eyes swivelling to the clock. It said 4.25. It was beginning to get light. The voice announced that it belonged to a police officer, calling from the station.

'Can you get down 'ere quick,' it went on. 'We are 'aving trouble with this g——.'

I did not catch the last word of his sentence. It sounded like 'ghost'. Yes, very likely, I thought. Oh yes, a ghost at the police station. Let's put one over on the new RSPCA inspector on his first night. Very funny.

'All right,' I said. 'Thanks for the welcome. Can I go back to sleep, please, now you've had your joke.'

'It's no joke,' cried the policeman, 'there's this bloody goose and it won't let anyone near the station. It's attacking anyone who tries to get past it. You're the expert, so come down 'ere quick, will you.'

'Right,' I said, waking up fast, 'I'll come straight away.'

I pulled some trousers and a sweater over my pyjamas and went out to my van. I drove to the police station, the route taking me down a hill to the sea front and then along the promenade. There I found a posse of police officers who had been trying in vain to report for duty at the station.

'It's up there on the left,' a sergeant told me, pointing. Men were still swarming towards us as I got out of the van and peered in the direction he had indicated. It was obviously a big event in the life of this particular police force, and it seemed that I was as much an attraction as the goose. The new man on his first assignment – how would he cope?

Then I saw it. This big white goose. This monster that had turned the might of the law to jelly. At that moment a young constable decided to make a run for the station steps. He set off, all dash and determination, as if he was about to score the winning try at Cardiff Arms Park with a magnificent curving sprint; a few seconds later he was backing up as fast as he could go, turned back by the goose which had charged across with a sudden burst of speed, in the full-back role, hissing, its wings outstretched, cutting him off from his target and leaving him nowhere to go except backwards.

Now, it seemed, it was my turn. From behind the shelter of my van, crouching figures looked expectantly towards me. I nodded, accepting that the challenge was rightfully mine, and did an urgent mental flip through the RSPCA file which I had recently opened in my memory. What had they taught me at training college about getting to grips with a homicidal goose? The reply came back quickly: nothing. Ah, but wait, there *was* something. That old chief inspector, he had shown us how to handle a swan, would that be any use? 'Get them by the neck,' he had said, 'then they are helpless.'

I stepped out from the cover of my van, assuming an air of nonchalance which was entirely false. 'He's all yours, Jenkins, boyo,' came an encouraging voice from behind me. At least they know my name, I thought. But what would my name be worth five minutes from now? Would it be a symbol of glorious action, the stuff of future legends in that part of the country, or would it, more likely, be mud?

I edged forward in the direction of the goose. It spread its wings and gave out an almighty hiss. I stood my ground, and a deadly silence fell over the promenade, interrupted only by the hisses of the goose and the swishing of its feathers. The audience was waiting for the novice to do his stuff; a shiny, bright new career hung in the balance.

'Come on, my girl,' I said, looking as stern and brave as pretence would allow. 'I'm not afraid of you.' It was probably the biggest whopper I had told in my life. By then we were about a foot apart, but the goose had not made its expected onslaught. 'Get them by the neck,' the old chief inspector's voice came to me again. I lunged forward.

The goose reacted by dodging to one side. I missed the neck but my hand caught her a smack across the beak. Without thinking I immediately shouted: 'Right! That's enough. Come here!'

What happened next was incredible. It seemed that the smack on the beak really had shown this powerful creature who was the boss. She waddled up close to me, as placid as a lamb. I stroked her beak to reassure her, and she appeared to love it. In the background I heard gasps of awe issuing from the watching policemen.

Something inside me told me I was on to a winning streak. I pushed my luck still further and ordered the goose to follow me. 'Right! This way.' I waved my arm and to my great relief and the wonderment of all, she did just what I wanted. I could have kissed her. The door of the station was opened wide, policemen stepped back to make way for us and we marched up to the desk. I asked the sergeant for a cell to accommodate my feathered friend until I could get her more permanent accommodation at a local bird sanctuary. Two minutes later the goose had stepped into a cell and peace was restored to the police station.

'I'll be back later this morning to pick her up,' I said, as though the incarceration of dangerous geese was all part of an average day's work. I turned to leave, and now the congratulations flowed. Someone pushed a mug of tea into my hand, people patted me on the back and I bathed in a sudden shower of compliments. This would do very well as my 'welcome in the hillside', I thought.

The case of the errant goose was not yet completed. Back at home I searched through my possessions, still scattered round me in unpacked cases and tea-chests, for a particular book which explained how to transport birds. Finding it at last, I read: '. . . take a sack and cut a hole in the closed end just large enough for the bird's head to be put through. This will allow the sack to be pulled down over the wings and when tied will prevent damage to the plumage.' That seemed to answer my needs. I allowed myself the luxury of a two-hour snooze.

Later that morning I reappeared at the police station, carrying a sack. I had decided to call the goose Belinda. How was she getting on? I asked, and was told that she had been pretty vocal but recently had quietened down. I approached the cell door. I could have done with a volunteer to come into the cell with me, but suddenly no one was free; men who had been standing around were now studying bits of paper, in an absorbed manner, or walking briskly away. I went in alone.

'Now, Belinda,' I said, 'look what I've got for you.'

Belinda's gaze swept over the sack and she evidently decided that it was not for her. As I went forward, she stepped briskly back, then moved to one side. I followed, she dodged the other way. I cornered her, she threatened me with hisses. I coaxed her, she didn't want to know. This went on for about ten minutes, neither of us getting anywhere. There was only one thing for it. I threw away the sack.

Now I went up close to the goose, reached out and gave her a quick tap on the beak. Immediately, Belinda calmed down. It had worked again. Wondering if my luck would hold a second time, I opened the cell door and, stroking her beak once more for luck, gave the order and we marched out together through the police station to my van. Ahead of us ran a young constable, opening doors as we came to them. The rear doors of my van stood open and so, giving that lovely beak a final pat, I said: 'Right. In you get.' And Belinda, bless her, hopped smartly aboard, to the further amazement of our audience.

A few days later I was able to assess more fully the impact of what had happened. A newcomer in the community, I went into a local pub and there in the taproom the welcome mat was well and truly laid down. I was met with nods and smiles all round. 'There you are, boys,' said an old-timer, pulling on his pipe, 'it's Jenkins the Goose.'

CURSING IN THE HILLSIDE

A not-so-warm welcome awaited me at the farm of Brian Davies and Mary Gorman. Not, that is, if you don't like being shot at.

I had been in West Wales about two weeks when I went to investigate a farm up in the hills. Someone had reported that a lot of dead sheep were lying unburied on the property. I went up there with a police sergeant, and a quick look-around revealed plenty of evidence. What was going on? The sergeant and I went over to the farmhouse.

Brian Davies had two brothers who farmed further down the road, and he and Mary Gorman (not their real names) worked this particular farm together. I do not think there was any emotional link between them, it was just a business arrangement.

Our first attempt at holding a conversation was highly unpromising. 'I am Inspector Jenkins from the RSPCA,' I said, 'and I have come about your sheep. . . .'

I was standing a few yards from the house, having stopped there when the front door opened and a man I took to be Brian Davies emerged, followed by a woman. In one hand he grasped the stock of a shotgun. I introduced myself and the response was immediate. Up came the gun.

'Get off my land, damn you!' shouted Davies, and fired a round over our heads to emphasize his point.

'Nice welcome we've got here,' I muttered to the police sergeant.

Somehow we stood our ground, and by keeping calm and talking persistently to them we managed to advance towards the couple. The gun was put down and eventually we were admitted to the house.

It was not the sort of place you would want to stay at for your summer break in the country. It was old, rickety and dirty, and at least a couple of centuries behind most people's houses in terms of creature comforts. There was no gas or electricity, and they had calves and cows living in part of the house; the smell was unbelievable. The farmers' own sanitary arrangements were limited to a large tin with a hole in the top. Their diet seemed to consist of cold baked beans and pears.

The state of the farm, unfortunately, reflected that of the house. The animals had not been properly fed, when they were fed at all, and many of them had died, their bodies being left, unburied, where they dropped. We had to take action against the farmers; there was a court case and they were convicted.

The woman, Mary Gorman, resented us from the start, perhaps even more deeply than the man – and she had a scary way of showing her feelings. In the course of that first visit she laid a curse on me. 'You will never smile again,' she suddenly swore, glaring at me with wild eyes.

I got back at her quickly. 'You will never know another day's happiness,' I said.

Her face went completely white. She knew, as I did, that I had undone her curse by laying one on her. Also, because I had done this, she would not, according to the local laws of witchcraft, be able to put a second curse on me. Victory in the war of superstition was mine – and she did not like it one bit.

During the next few months I had to make many visits to the farm to collect evidence and to check on the improvements we had ordered them to make. One of these concerned the burial of dead animals, and even here I met with fierce resistance from the farmer.

I had another police sergeant with me this time, and I was doing the talking. 'Look,' I was saying, 'you've *got* to do it. Why don't you just get on with it?'

'I'm not doing it,' Davies kept saying, to my intense frustration. 'You can't prove these are all my animals. . . .'

I was getting nowhere. Then the sergeant, a very experienced man nearing retirement age, offered to try on my behalf. I agreed and stood back while he had a word with the farmer. They talked for some little while, and I saw the sergeant pass something to the other man.

That was it. The farmer nodded and walked away from us, and minutes later he was picking up the dead animals and burying them. I turned to the sergeant:

'What did you do?' I asked him. 'Why has he changed his mind?'

The sergeant gave me a wise look. 'With people like him it's best if you don't give orders. They are very obstinate. He said some of the animals weren't his, so I agreed with him and asked him to do it for us as a favour. I gave him a couple of bob as well. We won't have any more trouble with him.'

He was right. The argument was over, and all the dead animals were duly buried by the farmer. Still, I could not help thinking as we drove back to town: there *are* some funny people round here. As well as geese.

ANIMAL SQUAD

In August 1983 I met Paul Berriff for the first time when he appeared at our Group Communications Centre in Leeds. It was a meeting which was to change my life dramatically.

Paul is a documentary film maker, and with him was Judith Stamper, a news reporter from the BBC Television *Look North* programme. Their assignment that day was to cover a disturbing story about the charred remains of a cat which had been found and which I suspected had been the victim of a ritual sacrifice.

I had already contacted various newspaper people about this story, but they had been less than keen to follow it up. Their view was that the pictures would be too disturbing and horrific for their readers. However, Paul and Judith agreed with me that it was the kind of story which ought to be put before the public. We went to work, and the story appeared as a news item that same evening. Much more was to follow.

Paul has won many awards for his documentary work, which includes individual films such as *Gold from the Deep* and series such as *Rescue Flight*, *Motorway Police* and *Lakeland Rock*. As we prepared the news item, I filled him in on the various tasks we undertake in our RSPCA Group. Like many people, he had tended to think of us as an organization mainly concerned with running animal homes for stray dogs and cats. I was able to show him that we in fact tackled a great range of investigative work as well, through our national network of inspectors. In effect, although our numbers are much smaller, we operate on lines similar to the police. We carry out methodical and painstaking investigations which may involve us in stake-outs, road blocks and all kinds of undercover work.

Paul was soon fascinated and wanted to know more. We arranged some further meetings, and I told him about our methods and how we deal with our heavy work-load, which every year increases at a most worrying rate. I also described some recent cases we had been involved with, and Paul became convinced that here was a 'natural' for a television film. Over the next eighteen months he and I met several times to plan what we wanted to do, and on the basis of these talks Paul put together a synopsis for a film. We took this down to RSPCA Headquarters in Horsham, Sussex, and received the necessary permission to go ahead with our project.

The next task was to pre-sell the film to a television company. Paul found sympathetic ears at the BBC and was commissioned to make a forty-minute documentary for BBC1.

So it was that in the late summer of 1985 a film crew attached itself to my life. Where once in my home on the outskirts of Leeds I was one half of a household, and my wife Sue the other half, now we were five. Five of everything became the standing order, and extra cuppas issued from our kitchen in an apparently endless flow.

Paul Berriff was the cameraman as well as the producer-director, and to help him he had Ray Parker, soundman, and Jon Pinkney, assistant cameraman. In the company of these dedicated professionals I learned a great deal about the techniques and practices of film making, which up till then had been an uncharted zone for me. At first my new colleagues pointed things out to me politely: could I not rattle those keys or loose change in my pocket; could I put my tie back on, please, for the next scene so as to keep the continuity – that kind of thing. I learned to live with a radio microphone about my person for long periods, and took care not to say anything rude about the crew during that time because they were listening to everything I said. As I warmed to the work, they were kind and tolerant towards my practical jokes, all of which they had seen before, e.g. flushing the toilet and holding the microphone close to the cistern – the effect on the soundman's ears is amazing!

The more we got to know each other, the better we fitted together as a team. Soon enough, we were on shouting terms; when you can shout at someone in the heat of the moment and know that they will understand and react positively, then you have a good working relationship. This applied equally to my RSPCA colleagues, the Inspectors and Co-ordinators of RSPCA's Group Two, Region Eight. They too were essential players in the *Animal Squad* team, and they too were happy to accept the film crew as sympathetic and caring professionals.

Incidents were filmed as they happened. From the moment we were called out on any of the investigations, Paul used his camera as a fly-on-the-wall, recording without commentary the scenes as they unfolded. In the course of our first three months together we compiled an extraordinary mass of material, some of it disturbing, all of it illuminating and to my mind made particularly vivid because we did not comment or preach but simply showed the viewer what was there.

It soon became apparent to Paul that we had far more material than could be fitted into one forty-minute programme. He took the first rushes along to Roger Mills, Head of Documentaries for BBC1, and won a new agreement – to make a series of six thirty-minute films.

The finished episodes of *Animal Squad* truly reflected the variety of our work: from issuing a reprimand to the owners of a dog abandoned in the family car on a hot day without proper ventilation, to the horrific neglect which we uncovered at a battery unit where hundreds of hens had been left to die and decay on top of one another in the most appalling conditions. Elsewhere, we filmed the sad last days of a run-down zoo; the story of a fox living in a concrete bunker on a housing estate, and his eventual return to the wild; the fate of a starving dog we were too late to save; strange goings-on in the house of a witch; days on the trail of a badger-baiting ring, and several shorter incidents which we filmed in the city and on various farms.

The response to the series was immediate and fantastic. When the *Animal Squad* programmes appeared, in the autumn of 1986, I not only found myself for the first time in the full glare of the public eye, I also found that my work-load, and that of my colleagues, was rising at an alarming rate as hundreds of people rang in with new complaints. To our great gratification, the programmes had obviously established a bridge between the RSPCA and the public, large numbers of whom now had a much clearer picture of what we actually did. They were also very appreciative of the fact that we could be trusted to protect an informant. In many people's minds a fear was lifted once they realized, through watching the series, that the RSPCA would never divulge the identity of someone who came forward to report a case of cruelty to an animal.

Phone calls poured in to RSPCA Group Communications Centres all over the country. We in Leeds, being the 'home' team, received our fair share of extra calls, and our lives have not been the same since. We have been working longer hours to try to cope with the extra burden, but the investigations just keep piling up on our desks. In the first quarter of 1987, for instance, we were to deal with some 300 separate complaints of cruelty; in the same period in 1986 (before the television series) we had about 200 complaints. As a total, that may not sound huge, but if you think that one serious investigation can involve many hours of work spread over a period of months, then you can perhaps see the extent to which we are now stretched. In the next chapter I explain in more detail the scale of our problems and how we try to cope with them. Meanwhile, there is a personal angle too, and it has made an immense difference to everything I do.

I now receive so many requests to give talks to every imaginable kind of gathering, I could be booked up every day or night for a year ahead if I accepted them all. Some of the people who ask me don't seem to realize that I have a job to do as well, and that I can only take on a limited number of outside commitments which I have to fit in as best I can in my free evenings or at weekends.

In a quite unexpected way I have become a spokesman for the animal population. Whether it's for television, radio or the newspapers, nowadays if a frog sneezes the reporters ring *me* up to find out why. It doesn't matter that the frog didn't sneeze on my patch of Yorkshire territory, it's me they come to for a quote. I am happy to do what I can, but just lately it has been almost overwhelming. Partly this is because callers don't understand how small an organization we are and what few resources we possess. For example, there is a tendency for the press and others to ring our Group Communications Centre and then, finding that I am not there, they ask if I will ring them back. It may be all right for them, perhaps, to run up telephone bills regardless of the expense, but the RSPCA is a charity and we simply can't afford it. I don't say that because I am in any way looking for an excuse not to co-operate, but just so that more people may realize that they need to be a little bit more understanding. If I am out, it's because I am working, and I may not be in a position to respond to a new caller for several hours.

In the long term, I am sure, all this attention will be for the good. For my colleagues and myself it is very important that we maintain this wider relationship we have been able to form with the public, and keep on pushing home our message so that more people than ever learn what the RSPCA is about, call us with animal problems which concern them, and support us whenever possible with their donations.

There is at the moment far too much cruelty being inflicted on animals, both in Britain and overseas, and it is essential for us that we do not allow the momentum of our campaign against it to drop. Ultimately, the way to beat all this cruelty is through education. The more we can promote our cause, the better our chances of creating a healthier public attitude towards animals. This can lead to more *prevention* of cruelty, which is our main function, and less of having to clear up cases after the cruelty has been committed.

work on similar lines is planned for the future. I am looking out for the day when we begin to see a real change for the better in the way animals are treated. That, far more than any personal fame, will be our best reward.

Can You Send One of Your Men?

I don't know how many policemen there are in Leeds, but I do know there are more than one. If only I could say that about RSPCA inspectors.

In the whole of my Group, which covers most of West Yorkshire and part of North Yorkshire, there are six inspectors. In the whole of England and Wales the RSPCA Inspectorate consists of 240 uniformed officers. Every working day things happen to remind us what a small organization we are and how limited in our resources.

One of the most common reminders is when someone rings up to report a case of cruelty. 'Can you send one of your men?' they say. But there is only you. Difficult; especially at night, when the duty inspector who receives the call in his own home must stay at his post all night. If a case comes through which requires immediate attention he has to consider waking a colleague in his Group and sending him to investigate. After midnight, in particular, this is a grind that most would rather do without; next day is a working day for them in any case, and will arrive soon enough. For the rest, the duty man hopes that he can get by until 9.30 next morning, or Monday morning if it is the weekend, with words of advice and encouragement or by calling on the help of other agencies such as veterinary surgeons, the police and the fire brigade, depending on the nature of the problem.

As you can perhaps imagine, there are drawbacks to all these long spells of duty, which can be very hard on the individual. It goes with the job that our inspectors work remotely and by themselves for much of the time, and they are expected to use their own judgement as to how they organize their time to deal with the various complaints passed on to them. One problem with such a system is that there can be no harder taskmaster than oneself, and people are inclined to push themselves more than they should. They are always overworked but they are often unwilling to take time off which is due to them. 'I can't,' they say, meaning that they would rather push on and try to catch up with the backlog of work piled up on their desk. That is all very worthy and I understand the reasons for it. But if people don't take time off to rest and recharge, they eventually slow down out of fatigue and everything gets on top of them; then they become ill and are forced to take time off.

From my own experience I know that my men must have a day off now and again. We are so thin on the ground already, we can't afford to have people off sick for the simple reason that someone else then has to try to fill in for them and we all drop further behind.

There is another drawback which is potentially much more dangerous, particularly for inspectors based in our big cities. Because they have no one else to back them up they have to walk alone into districts where a policeman would not go by himself. The day before writing this, I had to serve a summons in an area where I know that the policemen always go in twos. I claim no heroics for this; it is a risk we have to take. My nearest colleague is in Bradford, and he has enough on his plate without having to come over to Leeds and hold my hand while I serve a summons in a dodgy street.

It would also be inexcusable if an inspector were to discriminate between one part of his territory and another, avoiding calls to difficult areas and favouring visits to 'nice' streets where people were less tense and more polite. All calls must be treated with equal care and concern, regardless of their origins.

Some of the initial complaints we receive are undoubtedly trivial, but at that early stage we do not try to judge their merits. Very few complaints, by the way, are trivial to the person who makes them.

Every call that comes in during the daytime to our Group Communications Centre in Leeds is first of all taken down and logged by the co-ordinator on duty. This is the job of one of our two girls, Ruth Markinson and Trish Brown, who work a one-week-on and one-week-off system between them.

Whoever is on duty then notifies the inspector in the relevant area by radio, and he has to go out and investigate the complaint. As I have mentioned, I look after the Leeds area and there are five other inspectors responsible for their own territories. In Bradford is Inspector Dave Millard, who also deputizes for me when I am on leave or away on duty. At Skipton in the Yorkshire Dales is Inspector John Oxley; his area is mainly rural and he is usually to be found around the farms or at the cattle market. Huddersfield is the base of Inspector Kevin Manning, and provides him with a mixture of town and country work, and not far from him in Halifax is Inspector Derek Woodfield. Over to the north of Leeds, Inspector Stephen Wilkinson was based in the town of Harrogate and he looked after this and the surrounding countryside. (He has since left the Society to become a dog warden at Bradford.) Naturally, with such a wide area to cover between us, radio is a much better method of communication than the telephone, and each inspector's vehicle is equipped with its own radio so that he can receive calls while he is out and about and no time is wasted hanging about his base waiting for the telephone to ring.

Only when an inspector arrives on the scene of a complaint is he really able to assess how serious it is. Some complaints are either wrong-headed or malicious – the product of a quarrel between neighbours, for instance, where one family notices that the other lot are leaving a dog tied up in the garden, so they decide to report it just to bring them a bit of trouble and embarrassment. The inspector, of course, has no way of knowing what is going on until he can actually see for himself.

How then, you might say, can an inspector spot a real emergency and get there in time to deal effectively with it? This, I have to agree, is not easy; there may be nothing about a particular situation, as it is described on the phone to our co-ordinator, which makes it stand out from any other of the many calls received that day. On the other hand, there may be *just* some little detail which is odd, or different, and attracts the attention of the co-ordinator who can then say to the inspector: 'This one sounds a little bit special.'

Fortunately, most RSPCA inspectors manage over the years to cultivate an extraordinary ear for a crisis. Passing a verbal complaint on to them is a bit like showing a suspect package to a sniffer dog. If something is wrong, he will pick it up; a tiny mechanism goes 'ding!' inside his head, alerting him. That is all, but it is enough. Now he *knows* that this is a priority case and he should get there as quickly as he can.

Just the other day I experienced an instance of this myself. A dog had been abandoned, then found by someone else and handed in to the Animal Home in a poor state. Now, on this occasion we actually knew where the owner of the dog lived. Something, somehow, made me think very carefully about that. Perhaps, I asked myself, there is another animal in the house? There was no *reason* why this should be so, I just felt it fitted these particular circumstances. I therefore decided to follow up what my instinct told me, and so I went to the house. There I found a cat whose eye had been punctured. I took the cat into care, and later in my report to the RSPCA HQ I was able to make out a very strong case for prosecuting the owner for cruelty to both the dog and the cat.

Another problem with special or emergency cases is that they can be very time-consuming. If an inspector begins his day's work by investigating an emergency or special call, he may well find that nearly the whole day has gone by before he is able to look at anything else. Meanwhile, another animal's health may have deteriorated, and this case too will have turned into an emergency, or worse, by the time the inspector has got round to investigating it. Sometimes you just can't win. In fact I have never had a day yet when I managed to do what I had planned the previous evening – and I make a plan for every single working day. The only thing an inspector can try to do is to make his planned start (provided nothing else has turned up in the meantime) and then be prepared constantly to reassess the priority of the complaints and other demands which then queue up for his attention.

Say you get a report about dead sheep. How important is that? Someone rings in to say that several sheep are lying dead in a field near such-and-such. This is the kind of case which needs to be dealt with as soon as possible, for various reasons which I will explain in a moment. However, it cannot be classed as an urgent matter because the animals are dead, and there is no element of suffering. Our priorities must always favour the animal which is alive and suffering; it may be on the way to dying, no matter what we do to try and save it, but as long as it is suffering we must try to relieve its pain.

Obviously it is the farmer's responsibility to inspect his sheep regularly and bury any dead ones promptly to prevent the spread of disease, but these are tasks that sometimes are neglected. The law requires dead sheep to be buried in a 'reasonable time' and this rather vague limit is open to abuse. In the *Animal Squad* series we filmed at a farm where the sheep in one field varied from decomposing corpses to recently dead animals and others that were severely lame. When we questioned the farmer he admitted that he did not go up to that part of his land more than once a fortnight, and even if that were true he must have failed to notice at least two dead sheep on his previous visit. We prosecuted this farmer and he was fined £250.

If dead sheep are left, it is all too easy for other sheep to pick up a disease which then spreads through the farm and on to neighbouring farms. Dogs may try to eat from the carcass, which is another danger, as is the possibility that crows will peck out the eyes of a dead animal and drop them in another field. Pecking out the eyes is a habit with crows and they don't waste much time about doing it.

All these reasons make it important for us to deal with dead sheep as quickly as we can. At the same time we have to accept that the needs of the case are not as pressing as they would be if we were dealing with a suffering live animal.

Amid all these investigations and shifting priorities, the RSPCA inspectors have to fit in their routine work: visiting cattle markets, horse sales, pet shops, slaughterhouses, breeding establishments. Then there are the road checks, when the police ask us to help them examine vehicles carrying livestock. These checks are carried out by traffic examiners who measure the loads of heavy vehicles on a weighbridge and generally assess them for safety. With lorries carrying animals, it is the RSPCA's job to look after the animals' welfare during the check, and also to see that they have been loaded properly and without overcrowding.

This is routine work – patrolling rather than investigating – but we cannot push it to one side; it all has to be done. Then there is the educational side, which some may say is ultimately the most important branch of all the things we do. People ask us to go to schools and give talks, teaching children to respect animals and treat them properly as pets. I enjoy these visits and make them as often as I can, sometimes in the company of my own cat, Landy, who has turned out to be a great ambassador for us (see 'Landy, Our Champion').

Recently a new network of Project Offices has taken some of

these duties from us. This is a scheme run by the Manpower Services Commission in conjunction with the RSPCA. Project Offices are being set up in a number of our cities and the officers are already beginning to carry word of our work into the schools on a much bigger scale than we could ever have managed by ourselves. I am glad that this scheme has been started and wish it well in the future. There is so much that can be achieved with children, especially if they can be approached early in life and encouraged to give a little thought to their pets and other animals, to wonder about the 'why' as well as about the 'how to'.

We also have our local RSPCA branches to consider. Each uniformed inspector works within a branch area which is autonomous within the Society. My branch is called Leeds and District and each of my Group colleagues has his own local branch to which he reports and which acts as an information and fund-raising centre for members living in the area. Each RSPCA branch, in conjunction with its supporting auxiliary units, or sub-branches, organizes its own fund-raising efforts and pays a quota of its receipts to HQ in Horsham, Sussex. I make a point of popping in regularly to see my branch secretary and attending branch committee meetings at which I explain what I have been doing on their behalf.

One of the most important aspects of the branch's work is running the RSPCA's Animal Home. In Leeds our Animal Home has kennels for a hundred dogs, a cattery, a clinic and a boarding establishment for when people go away and their pets need temporary accommodation. The Animal Home is run by a manager and ten full-time staff, and its functions are quite distinct from my duties as a uniformed inspector.

We work together regularly, of course, often when an animal has been badly treated and is taken into care at the Animal Home. It then stays there while its future is sorted out, and perhaps another permanent home is found for it. From time to time I also persuade people to attend the clinic at the Animal Home so that their pet can receive proper veterinary treatment. This often happens when the owner is close to breaking the law, out of ignorance as well as from neglect, and I ask him or her to attend the clinic as a means of getting the animal fit – and also as a means of demonstrating to the owner where he or she has not been providing adequately for the animal's needs.

This is an essential part of my work. I would much rather say to someone: 'Look, your animal needs treatment and you need advice' than start court proceedings against them. Prevention is the aim of the Society, not prosecution. If I can get them to agree to go down to the clinic and see the vet for as many times as he wants to see them, I count this as a victory for the animal and its future. Mind you, it is not always an easy business to get a wayward pet owner, perhaps an elderly person who is a little bit confused at the best of times, to do exactly what you ask them. The clinic is where you can hear conversations such as this:

Vet: 'Have you brought that sample of your dog's water?'

Owner, after much fishing in shopping bag: 'Yes, here it is.'

Vet: 'Thank you. I'll just test this right now.'

Minutes later, Vet in a puzzled voice: 'I'm not getting any result. How did you say you took this sample?'

Owner: 'I got it from t'kitchen tap. He drinks t'same as we do.'

Ah, well. One does what one can. The important thing with all pet owners and people in charge of larger numbers of animals, such as farmers, is to secure their goodwill. Diplomacy is the number one asset in the mental make-up of an RSPCA inspector.

Going wider than the branch and its activities, there are many other people and organizations with which I must liaise all the time and keep a good relationship going. They include the local vets, the police, the fire brigade, as well as contacts at the newspapers and the radio and TV stations. You need to be on good terms with all of these people because you never know when you will next be asking one of them to do something for you.

So much of what we members of the Inspectorate do, and how we do it, is governed by the fact that we are by and large on our own. The Group Communications Centre, as I have explained, handles the incoming calls between 9 a.m. and 5 p.m. and relays the complaints to the local inspectors for investigation. At 5 p.m. each day the duty inspector, having done his day's work, takes over and receives all the calls for the Group at his home, where he stays until 9.30 the next morning; he then goes out again to do another day's work. That evening, another inspector takes over the night duty and this system operates until the weekend.

At weekends, a different duty inspector takes over at 5 p.m. on

Friday and handles all the calls until 9.30 on Monday morning. Each weekend call is considered carefully, and the nearest local inspector then goes out to investigate where necessary. Every inspector – including the Chief! – takes his turn at night and weekend duties. In our Group the weekend turn should come up once every six weeks, although at the time of writing we are a man short so it's every five weeks.

The product of all these complicated rotas is that each RSPCA Group is able to provide a live voice to the public, offering advice and a personal visit where necessary, and it does this twenty-four hours a day, every day of the week. For a charity to be able to run such a service, especially a charity as small as ours, is in my view nothing short of brilliant.

Obviously there are times when we find it very hard to cope. We do not have resources beyond the available inspectors of the Group, and it does happen, especially after midnight or if one of us is away or sick, that we don't have anyone to send and so must limit ourselves to acting as a telephone advisory service. At such times we ask people to be patient and do a little bit more for themselves. This is not our usual state of affairs, but it does occur. Equally, we do get people with funny ideas about what is important.

One night recently I was on night duty. I had one inspector on holiday and another way out in the hills searching for some sheep which had been injured in a road accident and had scattered all over the place. He would be out most of the night dealing with that crisis. I had just gone to sleep when a lady rang up. In an imperious voice she told me I must send a man round straight away – her budgie was on the roof!

I tried my best to explain that no one was available, but some people are hard to convince. The mere fact that you have answered their call makes them think that you are sitting in an office somewhere, with a cast of dozens if not thousands at your beck and call. If you try to suggest, however politely, that you can't drop everything just like that, they think you are making a feeble excuse. With this particular caller I tried to get her to see that, even if I *did* have someone to send round – which I did not – what could he really do that the lady and her husband were not doing already? The budgie, by her account, was in good health, and possibly wanted to stay out a little longer anyway, in which case it would be very optimistic, wouldn't it, to think that another human being would be able to climb up on the tiles in the dark and catch him.

She did not like it, I could tell. But there was simply nothing else I could do. I just hope the budgie flew down again next morning when he got a bit hungry. I say 'hope' because I never heard from the lady again. No news is not always good news, but in this case I reckoned it was.

Foxes in the City

They were once known as 'urban foxes', which usually meant that they lived on the fringes of a town. Now they are coming into the heart of our cities as well. Perhaps we should not be so surprised.

In the last thirty years we have built so many housing estates, industrial estates and motorway networks, we have destroyed many large areas which were once the natural habitat of our wildlife, places where they had lived undisturbed for centuries. Driven out of their homes and surroundings, they have come into our towns and cities to look for somewhere else to live. Among the animals now living wild within the city limits of Leeds are deer, foxes and peacock, and you can also find kestrels nesting in disused mills.

The foxes are the big colonizers: they have infiltrated along disused railway lines and settled themselves in quiet places like graveyards, where they know they are rarely disturbed at night. It is not uncommon to see a fox out on a raid for food, and, of course, they carry with them a certain reputation for ruthlessness and savagery. Much of this, I suspect, is based on tales we learned in childhood rather than on first-hand observation. However, it has not stopped a new wave of folk tales from circulating, in which the fox sneaks in from the countryside and kills and eats someone's cat.

In my experience, you are more likely to find a fox and a cat sitting quietly together, or else walking about and completely ignoring each other. It is usual for domestic animals to be curious about a newly arrived fox, and vice versa, but I have never seen a fox attack a cat. Dogs are the traditional attackers of cats, and I am sure that some of the stories I have heard are just plain wrong.

I know a lady who feeds foxes. At the back of her house she has a big expanse of grass which leads down to some woods. She puts out Yorkshire puddings for the foxes, having found that they like them very very much and are in fact on their way to becoming connoisseurs. Whether this is because they are Yorkshire foxes, she cannot say. At any rate, you can watch these foxes eat their puddings while cats from the neighbourhood go by, and there is never any conflict.

To me, foxes are more cat-like than dog-like. They have such spring in their legs, they can jump almost as high as a cat. In one of our *Animal Squad* films there is a marvellous sequence in which we have taken three foxes down to the RSPCA's special Wildlife Unit at Little Creech in Somerset. This was the first step in preparing them for release into the wild. When we arrived, we put the foxes into a pen to let them settle down, but settling down was far from their minds. They got very excited and started leaping about inside the pen, jumping six and seven feet into the air, straight off the ground, much higher than a dog would go.

VICKY

One little fox cub that came to us was found after a man had heard shots in a field. When he got there, the only living creature was this little vixen. In due course I arrived, gathered her up and drove back to our house, where my wife Sue took over the job of nursing her, as she often does with the wild animals that need special care after we have taken them in.

Vicky, as we called her, had to be bottle-fed – she was only a tiny scrap of a thing, and very young, a couple of weeks old at the most. Gradually we got some more life into her and she grew stronger.

At that stage it is important not to cuddle a wild animal too much and make it into a pet. Our task is to make it well enough so that one day it can fend for itself and be released back into its natural environment. So, with Vicky we were careful not to handle her too much; we gave her a little bit of affection now and then, but we resisted the temptation to take her on to our lap and stroke her.

A wild animal receives a lot from its natural mother that it is either difficult or impossible for we humans to provide. The mother's milk gives it immunity against certain diseases, for instance, and no substitute exists for that. The mother also teaches it things, such as how to hunt and sense danger. When feeding Vicky, we would sometimes pull the feed away in an effort to sharpen her awareness, to make her suspicious. Like most wild animals she was very quick to learn from this, building up by instinct a mental picture of how foxes live – a kind of survival kit for the future.

Another thing the mother provides is intensive grooming. In the wild she is continually licking and cleaning her young and looking after their coats. We can imitate the mother by cleaning and brushing the animal, but it is a very time-consuming business and sometimes we have to force ourselves to keep at it.

At first Vicky was so small, we kept her on a blanket. She was not strong enough to move about much, but once she was walking she soon became quite quick on her feet and we put her into one of our RSPCA animal modules, which is a special kind of metal cage with double doors. She came out for regular exercise and used to tear about the room, chattering as young foxes do. (They don't howl or yelp, as many people think; they give a little laugh, a strange kind of 'ha-ha-ha-ha-ha'.)

Our marmalade cat, Landy, was a bit put off at first, and spent long periods out in the garden. I think he was put off more by Vicky's scent than by the fact that she was a stranger or a possible rival. Foxes, however small, do give off a rather pronounced scent after they have been living in an earth.

Landy even fetched his friend, a cat called Morph who lives over the back. Together they used to sit outside on the patio with their paws up on the window, looking in at Vicky. It was almost as if they regarded her as a kind of entertainer. They sat there watching, not moving except for the odd slow swivel of the head, until Vicky went back in her cage, and then they pushed off up the garden to find something else to do. When Landy did come indoors, he and the fox got on perfectly well together and there was never any animosity between them.

Vicky stayed with us for six or seven weeks and then we took her down to the Wildlife Unit at Little Creech. By then she did not need special nursing: she was fit and well and ready to move on to the next stage – living in an enclosure. After that, she was put in a larger enclosure where she could learn to find her own food. Then, when she was seven or eight months old, and fully mature, she was released into the wild at a specially chosen location. The whereabouts of these locations are kept secret; they can be just about anywhere in Britain.

TWENTIETH CENTURY (FOX)

Twentieth Century was another visitor to our house. She was found in a lane in Leeds. She weighed 12½ oz (354 g) and was 9 in (23 cm) long. Her tail was thin and whip-like, and it was hard to imagine it ever growing into a proper brush.

In my notes on her I recorded that we fed her on a mixed diet of diced rabbit, minced catfood and diluted Carnation milk. In a very short time she weighed over 1 lb (about 0.5 kg) and grew stronger by the day. She 'killed' her blanket with enthusiasm, so we knew the hunting instinct was already alive in her.

Young animals come to us for a variety of reasons and it is not always easy to work out what has happened to them. Unlike Vicky, whose family were wiped out by someone with a gun, Twentieth Century was found wandering by herself. It was reasonable to assume she had been abandoned; we noticed that she was small, so perhaps her mother had recognized some deficiency and decided to reject her.

With us she not only survived, she did well enough to be taken down to Little Creech when she was fully grown, and eventually she was released into the wild.

PETER

Peter was reported to us by a man who had found him as a cub, abandoned on a patch of waste ground, and had taken him into his house. When I first saw him, Peter was about ten weeks old and clearly proving a handful. Foxes are not meant to be pets, as I said earlier, and I was able to persuade the man that he could not expect to keep Peter much longer. The best plan was to restore him to the wild.

I left Peter with his temporary guardian, promising to keep in touch. The next time I visited the house, about six weeks later, the fox's position was a lot worse than on my first visit. He had grown much bigger and stronger, so much so that he could not be kept in the house. The man had built a bunker of concrete and wire mesh for him in the backyard, concreting the floor so he could not burrow out.

That was OK, as far as it went, and at least the fox was having to rough it to some extent instead of being kept indoors like a household pet. The trouble was, the neighbouring gardens were home territory for several dogs, all of which were being driven frantic by the scent of this fox which they could smell but seldom see – and never get at. The dogs showed their feelings by barking and yelping for hour after hour, which not only put a strain on the nerves of all the people living in the surrounding houses, it also made the fox's life a perpetual misery. Most of its time was spent hidden away in the dark of its sleeping quarters at one end of the bunker.

It was clearly time to move Peter the Fox to more secure surroundings. With the man's co-operation, we brought him out of the bunker and I slipped a choke collar and lead over his neck. Together we set off for my van, while all around us the barking of the dogs became a great wall of fevered protest. Outside the gate one dog, on the loose, stood waiting for us, but I managed to keep him at a distance while I led Peter to the van and swept him quickly into the cage at the back. For the first time in his life, although he did not know it, he was safe from danger.

After a few days at the Leeds Animal Home, Peter was taken down to Little Creech with two other foxes which had been found in the Huddersfield area. One of these had been in the care of a policeman, who had kept it in his house, probably for too long. The policeman had even arranged for the fox to appear in a television programme; while they were at the studio, under the heat and glare of the lights, the fox turned on his keeper and bit him so severely in the face that he lost his sight in one eye.

I do not mention this in order to say 'I told you so', but the incident is further proof, surely, that an animal such as a fox does not exist in order to perform for the benefit of us humans. It belongs in the wild and should be returned there just as soon as it has learned, or re-learned, how to fend for itself.

FREDDY

He was an unusual fox in that he was already a victim of what you might call 'urban decay' before we came across him. He was found in a snare in a garden in Chapeltown on the outskirts of Leeds. Someone had set the snare to protect their chickens. Freddy walked into the trap and became ensnared; his howls were reported by a neighbour to the police and they called us in.

When we examined the fox, we found to our surprise that his teeth had gone rotten.

Freddy had been living in and around the town for so long, the soft food or leftovers that you find in dustbins had become the chief element in his diet. All this pappy food had made his teeth go soft and this in turn had forced him to abandon his natural habitat and take to the streets. Unable to kill for himself, he had become a kind of urban guerrilla.

He submitted rather unwillingly to a course of dental treatment, during which a couple of teeth were removed and the rest cleaned up, but for the remainder of his time with us he enjoyed more or less total luxury as a guest of the Leeds Animal Home. Being full-grown, and well practised in the arts of vagrancy, he was a crafty animal and difficult to handle. He would even steal from himself.

When we put food in his dish he would not accept that it was for him. His instinct told him to grab the food and take it into a corner and eat it there. We did not attempt to tame him or change his outlook. His view of things was precisely right for the future we had lined up for him, and in due course he too went down to the Wildlife Unit at Little Creech to be prepared for a return to the natural environment.

I sometimes wonder what became of Freddy, with his urban leanings and refurbished teeth. When released, did he immediately head for the nearest dustbin, or had the Wildlife Unit 'programmed' him sufficiently well that he had no need of soft options? Perhaps he even preferred to make an honest living for himself in some remote part of our countryside, and thrives there still? The most certain thing of all is that we shall never know the answers to these questions. And that is as it should be.

— ANIMALS HAVE MORE —
— SENSE —

Compared with animals, people are daft. We do the most extra-ordinary things to amuse and entertain ourselves, which no animal would ever dream of doing.

We go to the fairground and sit ourselves in the Big Dipper or the Catapult – in order to have a good time. We actually pay money to be half-blinded by flashing lights, half-deafened by over-amplified music and the screams of our fellow humans, while our own liver and lights are repeatedly flung up at the sky. It's quite incredible really. Ask any animal. 'Certainly not,' it would say. 'I'm not doing that. It's not natural.'

Think of what happens at the racecourse. We put a dozen horses and men into a race and thousands of people turn up to watch. You try putting the men into the race by themselves. You wouldn't get any horses to come and watch that, would you? Of course not. Animals have more sense.

Or do they? According to a lot of people, animals are great show-offs and really enjoy performing before a human audience. This is a popular plank in the argument which says that circus shows and suchlike are perfectly OK because the animals are having such a good time. I am not at all sure about this line of thinking.

To my mind, it is undignified for an elephant to have to walk on its hind legs or do a balancing act. 'Have to' is surely the test. Would an elephant, of its own volition, ever devise a routine in which it balances on one leg and perches a beach ball on the end of its trunk? I would be very surprised to find such skills being passed down from one generation of elephants to another with-out any interference from Man.

We humans, on the other hand, are different. Daft, certainly, as I have said, but there is more to it than that. We have our sense of adventure. We want to do things, like hang-gliding and parachuting, which are neither natural nor always necessary, and we do them *ourselves*. If something goes wrong, and we perhaps have a nasty accident, then we have nobody to blame but our-selves. It was our choice and our lookout. That is not at all the same as training an animal to do something that it would never think of doing by itself, in the wild.

I am also against the way animals are transported around from one place to another, be they cats or puppies in boxes, or rabbits in crates piled high on top of each other on the back of a lorry. Think also of circus animals, and the miserably small cages in which they are confined for long periods while the circus is out on the road. It is not only the physical discomfort that I object to; confinement such as this has a bad mental effect on animals, frightening them unnecessarily, making them nervous and more liable to become aggressive, and eventually, if it goes on long enough or is repeated too many times, changing their personality for the worse.

All the same, I have to be careful. It may be all right to criticize the training and transport of performing animals, but how far down the scale does 'performing' go? At Knaresborough Zoo (see 'The Trouble With Zoos') a lioness called Dandy-Leo had a famous trick of rolling over on her back like an enormous kitten. Where she learned to do this, I do not know; perhaps it was out of boredom, or perhaps she was taught by an animal trainer, back in her distant youth. But in any case, do we really need to worry about such things which, in Dandy-Leo's case, gave so much pleasure to her visitors?

Again, suppose it's your dog that does tricks. Suppose he sits up and begs for food, or carries the newspaper back from the shop. Does it matter that he can do these things?

It's a surprisingly knotty subject, the more you think about it, but in general my view is that animals should not be taught tricks. I would not teach a dog to beg. From there it is all too easy to get it doing all kinds of funny things, and that to me is wrong. Then, of course, there is my cat.

I am not entirely unaware that someone might say to me: 'Ah. But you allow your cat Landy to perform, don't you? You take it to exhibitions. You carry it round the country in a box, and you make it perform at cat shows.'

My answer to that is yes, to a certain extent you can say that we are putting him on show. But we are not asking him to do anything unnatural, since all he has to do at a show is to sit there and be judged. Meanwhile, we are promoting his welfare, and the welfare of other cats, by grooming him every day and doing all we can to make sure he is in the best possible condition when he is seen by others.

Each time he goes in for a show he is examined by a vet, so that's another safeguard, and then he appears before a panel of Cat Association judges who look him over very carefully and make out a written critique. If there was anything wrong with him, perhaps something we had overlooked, it would turn up in the critique, e.g. 'This cat has dirty ears.' Next time, we would make sure we remembered to clean his ears properly, and that can only be of benefit to the animal.

So, on balance, I feel we are not exploiting him. Taking a cat to a cat show cannot really be compared with training an animal to perform in a circus. There may seem to be one or two surface similarities, but when you look more thoroughly at the two, and their various requirements, I think most people would agree that they are not the same.

I would add just one more point. We always refer to Landy as 'him'. He is never an 'it', an object. He is a life, and deserves to be treated with respect. Each and every animal is a life, and has its own dignity, whether it be a dog or an insect. There is a tendency for people to exalt certain animals to the detriment of others, for instance to be sentimental – sometimes to an extraordinary degree – about horses, but at the same time to look down on cows and sheep as creatures not worthy of our consideration.

People ring us up to complain. 'So-and-so is keeping his horse out in the field at night, it must be ever so cold.' They don't stop to think that the horse may actually prefer to be outside, and they *never* ring up to complain about cows being left out, whatever the weather.

Why do we react in that way? There is certainly no logical reason to discriminate between a horse and a cow. I suppose one must accept that certain animals, through their appearance, are more popular with humans than others, but this is very much a matter for the individual beholder. In my time with the RSPCA I have been called out to investigate the condition of all kinds of 'unusual' animals: locusts, stick insects, snakes, a pet tarantula. I fully accept that such animals are less than universally appealing, and yet they all have a right to be treated humanely and with respect. If an animal – any animal – is in need of protection, it is our duty to cater for that need. It is the least we can do.

─Runners and Fliers:─ ─ Animals in Sport ─

When the playing career of a professional footballer comes to an end, he is usually able to switch into a second career. It may seem a bit of a come-down, after all those years of hurtling around in front of big crowds at Elland Road, Leeds, or somewhere like that, to find himself selling Mars bars to unruly kids over the counter of a Post Office & General Stores; but at least it's a living. Who knows, the ex-player may do a lot better for himself: get into television or sports management. Many things are possible nowadays. Either way, it's better than being a retired greyhound.

In Leeds they have shut the dog stadium, so we don't see as many greyhounds as we once did. I am glad about that, but every so often another one turns up, dumped by its owner once its racing career was over and it could no longer contribute towards its keep. Not all the abandoned greyhounds we take in are old dogs: some are turned out because they had an injury, or had merely stopped winning. Fate can be particularly cruel to an animal which has offended against the laws of profit and loss.

If we find a greyhound wandering out on the streets, the chances are that we will never be able to trace its owner despite the fact that most racing dogs are supposed to be 'tattooed' with an identification mark. So there it is, abandoned and in need of care. We accept it and look after it. Almost invariably it turns out to be friendly and highly intelligent. Given the chance, greyhounds make marvellous pets – as long as you don't have cats on the premises, because they will go for a cat. ('At last,' perhaps they think, 'a hare that isn't stuffed!')

In general though, the greyhound has a good temperament and makes a fine companion. It is sad that so many owners have no time or inclination to let this part of their relationship take root and develop. To my mind a greyhound should be owned for life, like any other dog. Owners who say they cannot afford this could easily reduce their commitment to the race track and give their old dogs a decent retirement.

Other animals in sport, unfortunately, are subject to a similar fate – or worse. When a racehorse breaks its leg, its whole future may be called into question: not just its racing future, but whether it should be allowed to live at all. Modern treatments are a great deal better than they were not all that long ago when it was common for a horse with a broken leg to be shot where it had fallen. To some owners, however, the fact that the leg can now be mended and the horse retired out has little appeal. He prefers to have it shot, because that way the animal is worth more to him. Then he can put in an insurance claim, and use the proceeds to buy another horse that he can race. Again, money is doing the talking.

The bond between animal and owner tends to be greater the more the partnership is removed from the world of bookmakers and prize money. With the small owner who jumps his horses at local events such as point-to-point races, the relationship is much closer and the animal is regarded more as one of the family. There is a parallel among dog owners: where man and dog work together as a team for their sport, you find that they are more likely to have a strong, life-long relationship. I am thinking of people who train sheepdogs, for instance, and take them round to compete in the various trials, or those who keep Whippets and Lurchers and go out lamping or poaching with them. The latter is not an activity I condone, by the way, but we would be deceiving ourselves to pretend it doesn't go on. (Lamping is where people go out hunting at night and use lamps to draw out their prey. You sometimes see advertisements in the local paper which say, for instance: 'LURCHER, exc. cond., used to the lamp. . . .' So now you know what they are up to!)

MISSING PIGEONS

I am regularly involved with racing pigeons that get into trouble. It is hardly surprising, given the nature of the sport and its huge popularity. At certain peak times of the year, I understand, there can be as many as twelve million racing pigeons in the air over Britain. As a result we can be inundated with people calling in about birds which they have found in a state of exhaustion. We then ask them to tell us the code on the bird's ring and by consulting our reference books we can establish the name of the club secretary. The finder then telephones him and reports that a bird has been found. Time and again, when the news is transmitted to the owner, he is not interested.

'Oh, aye,' he says. 'That's a young bird, isn't it? We don't want it. If it hasn't made its own way back, it's no good to us. Neck it.'

I think that is scandalous. If an owner tried to turn out a dog whenever he pleased, because he was tired of it or it had grown inconveniently large, he would soon have the law after him. A dog owner can be charged with 'abandonment in a manner likely to cause unnecessary suffering'. A pigeon-fancier would probably escape such a charge; not because pigeons are not protected in law but because it is difficult to prove unnecessary suffering in a bird when it is clearly able to fly and eat.

It is all very hard on the young, inexperienced pigeon. Inevitably some young pigeons will never make it as racing birds, but once a pigeon has completed a few races the attitude of these more flint-hearted owners undergoes a rapid change. If a bird is a three-year-old or older, and thus a mature racer, then they not only want it back, they want it back *quick*.

Meanwhile, who is bearing the cost of rescuing and looking after all these pigeons which have landed many miles from home? To the quiet delight of many pigeon-fanciers, it is the public and charities such as the RSPCA which are doing a lot of the groundwork, and I feel it is time that this was changed. The pigeon-fanciers could easily set up their own servicing stations to which birds could be brought when they were lost, sick or exhausted. At each centre arrangements could be made to send the bird back to the owner, who would be charged according to nationally agreed rules.

This would not be hugely expensive to set up, and the money could be raised without difficulty. If there are twelve million birds out racing on certain days of the year, an additional 1p on the ringing fee would go a long way towards funding a series of recovery stations.

People who want their sport should be prepared to pay for it. You can't expect to play golf without a set of clubs, so you buy or hire them. In sports where animals are involved, the administrators have an extra responsibility to make sure that *before* anything else is allowed to happen, the animals are adequately cared for. It's a small price to pay for all the pleasure they give.

DANCING BULL

How, when you are put on the spot, do you know what an escaped or cornered animal will do next? What can you do that will anticipate its next move and make it do what *you* want?

Not easy. Suppose you are called out to a farm because the bull is loose. You go out to recce the place and find that the bull, which had been running on the roads and frightening motorists, has now retired to a wood to think things over.

The chap who tells you this is a young, inexperienced farm manager, whose knowledge is obviously limited to what he has recently picked up at college. You can tell that he will be useless. Fortunately, he does not realize that you too are new to the job, as well as the area, but the other side of this coin is that he expects you to pull off what, in your terms, would be a miracle. And in five minutes.

Still, better do what you can. You did all right with the goose, didn't you? Right, now do it with a bull.

You gather half a dozen assorted onlookers and farmworkers together, and set off towards the wood. Everyone else goes into the trees armed with a stick, but you think, no, this would be against your never-cruel-to-animals image, so you go without (not very clever). The next half-hour is spent chasing the bull through the trees and round them, cornering it, losing it, and generally getting nowhere. The bull, a beautiful black-and-white Friesian, has definitely got the measure of his pursuers and could probably go on dancing about like this for a fortnight.

As you chase about, this way and that, you become aware that you are being watched. Someone is over there, an old boy, standing back from the action but taking in everything that happens, every lunge, parry and demoralizing retreat.

The more you keep looking out of the corner of your eye at this mysterious spectator, the more he seems to be amused by what you are doing, or not doing. Eventually you can no longer ignore the fact that he is laughing at you, so you go over to speak to him.

'You've been watching us,' you begin, finding it an effort to be polite. 'Do you know anything about bulls, then?'

'I've been with them all me life,' replies the old boy.

'Well, do you think you could deal with this one?' you ask, turning to look at the bull and the shaky cordon of helpers now surrounding it. For the time being the physical chase has been abandoned, and the humans seem to be trying to overpower the bull by firing dirty looks at it, which the bull is ignoring.

The stranger looks quietly scornful. 'I could do a darn sight better than you lot,' he says.

'All right,' you say, trying not to pull a horrible face. 'What are we doing wrong?'

'For one thing,' he says, 'you're chasing it. You should never chase bulls.'

'Oh. All right,' you say, giving in, 'do you know a better way?'

He nods, acknowledging your surrender. 'How about getting four cows and bringing them down here?' he suggests.

'What,' you say, 'and lose them as well?'

'No, no,' he says, patiently, 'that'll be all right. Just get your feller to bring four of his cows down here.'

So, after much debate and discussion with the farm manager, it is agreed. Four cows arrive, and the old boy goes to work. He drives the cows towards the bull and stops them. The bull immediately leaves the wood and comes over. The cows are turned about and driven back to the yard, and the bull follows quietly behind. No problem. End of drama.

Yes, you may say, that was very fine, but what is the *general* answer to the question at the beginning of this chapter? How *do* you deal with an escaped animal?

In my view there is *no* general answer. In this kind of work a lot depends on a person's experience. The thing I learnt from the episode with the bull was: if in doubt, don't be afraid to ask. There is always somebody who knows more than you do, and it may be better to spend your time finding the expert than to waste it running around trying to do the job yourself.

LEANING COW

I once saw a cow that looked as if its eye had been shot out. We were at a cattle market and I was on the point of calling in the police when I decided to ask an old boy for his opinion.

He gave the cow a quick glance. 'Don't worry about that,' he said to me. 'It'll be under treatment. It's got New Forest disease, which makes the eyes go like that. No need to worry, that should clear up.'

If he had not been there to tell me, I could well have jumped to the wrong conclusion, rung the police and told them they should start looking for someone who had been shooting at farm animals. What a waste of time and effort that would have been.

Of course, once you have learned something about animals – how they behave, the diseases they catch, and so on – it is important to try and remember what you have learned so you can reapply it later.

Since my days as a young boy in Leeds, helping the Warrington brothers on their farm, I have known that cows have a tendency to lean and pin you to a wall. If you are smart, you try to avoid becoming the filling in a cowshed sandwich, either by keeping away from the wall or by always, or whenever possible, having an escape route open.

A vet and I once rescued a Charolais cow that had fallen in a ditch. We had to use a tractor to pull her out, and then we took her back to the farm so she could be examined for any injuries. She was standing in the cowshed while the vet and I walked round her. Without warning she leaned sideways and squashed the pair of us against the wall.

'Thanks very much!' we gasped, after we had pushed and heaved our way out from under the vast pale flank. 'We get you out of the ditch and you do that to us!'

Ah, but we knew she would, didn't we? Cows have never shown much respect for people. Our trouble was, we had forgotten.

THE PUPPY FARMERS

In 1974 I received a complaint from someone in North Yorkshire asking me to look into the conditions under which Corgi puppies were being bred at a certain establishment in Wales. This was my introduction to a big and complicated subject: the breeding and transportation of puppies and dogs.

This man had bought his puppy at a pet shop in Bradford. When he got back to his home in Ripon it was soon obvious that there was something wrong with the puppy. It was sick and lifeless the whole time, and never showed any sign of getting better. The owner took it to a vet who after a brief examination wrote out the following report:

'This is to certify that I have this day, at the request of Mr X, living at [Ripon address], examined a red and white Corgi bitch, said to be nine weeks old. This pup was showing clinical signs of conjunctivitis, tonsillitis and pneumonia, which in my opinion is indicative of canine distemper. Apart from this the pup had clinical signs of rickets, and mange of the ear, fur, legs and abdomen.'

The Corgi's owner sent me a copy of the vet's report, and this and the further details of the case set me off on an investigation that lasted for three years. During that time I was appalled to find myself uncovering what amounted to a sordid cottage industry.

The main Animal Acts that were being flouted, as far as I could see, were the Pet Animal Act of 1951, the Animal Boarding Establishments Act of 1963, the Breeding of Dogs Act of 1973 and the Transport of Animals, Road and Rail Order of 1975. The requirements of these Acts are still being ignored today. Only recently I was called to Leeds City Station to look into a fifteen-hour ordeal suffered by three young puppies. They had been put on a train in Wales and were being sent to Bradford.

They were Border Collie pups, and they had been despatched on this long, arduous and frightening journey, without food, by the same man I had first investigated in 1974. Twelve years later, very little had changed.

While the establishments of these puppy farmers differed from each other in detail, many followed a similar working method. The owner was either a breeder or he set up a stud farm, to which people brought their bitches to be served by his dogs. He would then buy back the puppies, usually on the cheap, and sell them on to pet shops and dealers all over the country. The man in Wales was one of British Rail's biggest customers in the transport of animals by rail.

Ironically – or perhaps it is worse than that – he was chairman of the licensing committee of the local council which issued licences to breeding establishments and others in the area who dealt in pet animals. I discovered that he himself did not have a licence, and only after a great deal of discussion and argument did he agree to do something about it. 'I'd better get one,' was how he put it, none too graciously.

One of the shortcomings of the law at that time was that a breeder with two or more breeding bitches, whose puppies were offered for sale, had to have a licence and be registered. However, for someone with a stud dog a licence was not obligatory. This was the first excuse offered by the chairman of the licensing committee, despite the fact that he was freely committing all sorts of other offences at the same time.

During my first year as an RSPCA inspector in Wales I could get very little satisfaction from the council responsible. Despite meetings, telephone conversations and pleadings, it seemed to me that the law in these matters was looked on merely as a nuisance, which, provided they ignored it for long enough, might eventually go away.

Not surprisingly, this local council gained a reputation as a soft touch among animal breeders who were being pressed hard by more responsible councils elsewhere. As a result, more breeders started drifting into the area; one of these, Mrs Mountford let's call her, we will meet later.

I could see a pattern developing, and resorted to the media, especially the local newspaper, to attract publicity for my side of the argument. Looking back, it seems astonishing that I had to work so hard to prove points that were already covered in law. But that is how it was: the corruption was deeply entrenched and it took many months to convince people that I had incriminating facts about their activities and that I intended to use them.

During this time I had one important ally, a senior police officer who gave me a great deal of encouragement when I needed it most and who was also not afraid to act. Through his efforts, we got court proceedings started when the council would not act themselves. The case resulted in eleven convictions being recorded against the person accused, and it had the effect of severely embarrassing many of the council officers. It also led to some tightening-up among the breeding establishments, but we had a lot of work ahead of us because there were still plenty of dodges and loopholes that determined people could exploit.

One of the tricks used by the breeders was to slip into a litter a puppy that was not fully bred, thus giving it false credentials. This, I felt, was something the public should be made more aware of, so that people could protect themselves better when buying from dealers or pet shops rather than from legitimate breeders.

I was also disturbed to find that animals were being offered for sale by hire purchase. Two companies were offering voucher schemes which I thought were highly undesirable. The reason most people opt to pay for something by hire purchase is that they cannot produce the full amount in cash. That may be all right for something like a machine which has low or nil running costs, but pets are very much more demanding. They require a lot of maintenance, including attention at the vet's as well as regular feeding, and it seemed to me that people who could not afford to buy their pets outright would very likely be unable to maintain and feed them over their lifetime.

A well-known kennels was offering another service which I thought was very much against the animals' interests. This was a mail-order scheme which, with its built-in offer of 'your money back if not satisfied', could involve unwanted puppies in two long and distressing journeys by rail. In my report to HQ I recommended that the RSPCA should bring pressure to bear on all these practices.

ON THE TRAIL

To collect my evidence I travelled all over the place. On one occasion I followed a consignment of puppies that were being transported from Wales to Manchester. From Wales they travelled to Crewe where they were dumped on the platform in their crates and left for several hours. I sat with them, but there is not much you can do to console a group of lonely young animals packed up in an unpleasantly confined space.

The journey at last resumed, and we reached Manchester in the early hours of the morning. I sat with the puppies for the rest of the night, and then they were taken to a kennels which sells puppies to the public on the never-never.

The same man who sent those puppies to Manchester was also responsible for sending five Corgi puppies and three Poodles by rail to Great Yarmouth. On arrival, three of the Corgis were dead. This was verified by our local inspector who went to the railway station and saw them. The 356-mile journey took more than fourteen hours and included a road journey across London from Paddington to Liverpool Street. The puppies travelled in wooden crates of the tea-chest type, each measuring 2 ft by 1 ft 6 in (60 cm by 45 cm). Vents were let into the sides to give them air; all the same, it is a miserable environment in which to have to spend such a long period of time. In the opinion of the inspector, the puppies died from excessive heat.

People may say that you can get away with giving a dog one good meal a day, but puppies really need smaller feeds two or three times a day. They also need constant attention. To me it is wrong to subject such animals to a journey of this length. We tackled British Rail about it, and they said:

'In certain circumstances arrangements are made for feeding and watering particular types of livestock. However, in the case of small animals like puppies we do not make this provision; it would be impractical.

'Small animals are usually conveyed in strong boxes, and many such consignments are always in transit on British Rail. . . . The consignment carrying Corgi puppies was despatched by the 20.45 train from Carmarthen on Tuesday 5th August and arrived in Great Yarmouth at 11.20 the following morning. This was an excellent transit, particularly because cross-London transport was involved. There is no need to doubt that the livestock was fit to travel and it was certainly well packed. In the circumstances British Rail cannot offer any explanation as to why three puppies died.'

The fact remains, 'excellent transit' or not, three puppies died. Nor was that an isolated instance. We are constantly having problems with animals in transit, whether by rail or by road.

I will say that British Rail have tightened up their procedures and are now much more prepared to consult the RSPCA if they see problems arising. So far as puppies are concerned, the issue at the centre of it all is the nature of the trade. If people bought their dog direct from a legitimate breeder, and cut out the dealers or middle men, these dreadful journeys could be avoided. There would be no process by which the puppy is passed from its original breeder to a first dealer, such as the stud dog owner, who then sells it on to another dealer who sends it to a pet shop. If people bought direct, they would simply drive to the breeder and collect their animal themselves.

On the Farm: It's a Dog's Life

People who live in towns and cities would find it shocking if they saw some of the squalor and neglect that prevails in remote country areas. The popular image of a rural dog breeder's establishment would probably include a small farmhouse or a large cottage, all spruce and clean and perhaps with a thatched roof. To one side of the house would be a series of neat enclosures where the dogs were housed.

The reality is not like that. The reality is often a run-down bungalow with peeling paint and outhouses which are so derelict you cannot believe that any of them are in use. Here and there on the ground lie rotting carcasses of sheep, collected by the dog breeder from the farms where they died. They are now the chief source of food for the resident dogs which roam the property, unprotected and uncared-for. Inside the bungalow are more dogs, and these are kept in quite disgusting conditions. There is no control against disease, the dogs are not inoculated, and it is hardly surprising that many of them are in no state to be sold to the public.

Living in such squalid surroundings would get most people down after a while, and I began to notice that a number of the breeders I visited were finding it difficult to cope. One woman lived with an old aunt in a bungalow that looked quite presentable from the outside; the scene indoors was very different, however.

There were dogs in every room, about thirty animals in all. Several lived in packing-cases in the bathroom; the living-room was crowded with dogs, and there was excrement on the floor in every room. I went there with a vet one very hot summer day. The smell and the atmosphere were appalling. The central heating was on, and it was all I could do to stay on my feet.

The old aunt sat in a chair in the middle of all this, eating a sandwich. Dogs milled around her, yapping, no doubt hoping for a bit of the sandwich; one dog was peeing against her skirt. All the old woman did was to sit there and every so often cry: 'Shudderp. Shudderp!' To no avail. Fleas were everywhere. The place was hopping with them and, as we watched, they hopped on to us. When I complained to the owner, she replied:

'Oh, they're all right. They're better than wasps.'

Whatever that meant. As our eyes began to take in further details, I noticed that the only visible part of the woman's body that was clean was the backs of her fingers – which the dogs regularly licked for her. She later told us that she was entitled to live like a pig if she chose to.

With the vet's support I managed to get the woman to court, accusing her of causing unnecessary suffering to the dogs. We were able to prove that through her neglect the dogs were made to suffer because they had to inhale ammonia fumes from their own urine. We submitted that the conditions in which she kept her dogs were a scandal. She was fined £50, the maximum in those days, and ordered to pay £50.56 in costs. She was not banned from keeping dogs, but I watched her movements very closely over the next few weeks until she moved out of my area, having decided to try her luck elsewhere.

Another woman used a pub for breeding dogs. As far as hygiene was concerned, she had no standards at all. I saw a litter of puppies living in a grocery box in a filthy room, right next to where she cooked the pie and peas for her pub customers. The bar was in the adjoining room. As usual in such places, the smell was dreadful.

When I complained to the local council about these conditions, they did nothing. In the end I took the woman to court and got her banned from keeping animals. By this time her health had deteriorated. She had taken up with a drug addict and was not in control of herself. The dogs were bound to suffer even more than they had been doing, and one puppy had an eye poked out. That it was an accident, I am prepared to accept; but it could have been avoided if the council had taken action when I first complained to them.

The woman lost her pub licence through our intervention. She had to move out of the pub and went to live in a caravan. She stopped breeding dogs, and we at least had the satisfaction of knowing that more animals would not be made to suffer for as long as she remained out of business.

Not all breeding establishments are as capacious as the back room of a pub or the bathroom of a bungalow. One man, when we caught up with him, was breeding Sheepdogs in the back of a small van. He put a cardboard box in there for his bitches, and that was where they were expected to whelp. Naturally, some nights it was far too cold in the van, and when we at last caught him and investigated the vehicle, we found one puppy dead. I managed to get the local authority moving on this case, and they took the man to court for causing a health hazard.

This deterred him for a while, then he started up again. He was taken to court a second time, accused of causing unnecessary suffering to a dog. He still needs careful watching to this day. The experience of being taken to court wears off quickly on some people – though not on the majority, I am glad to say – and I am afraid he is the kind of man who all too easily slips back into his old ways.

'IF I'D MEANT TO SHOOT AT YOU, YOU'D BE DEAD'

When the word got round that a certain local council in my area of Wales were a soft touch for dog-breeders, one of the first new arrivals was a lady we will call Mrs Mountford. She had come all the way from Kent, where the authorities, rightly, had been giving her a hard time. She arrived in a hired van with thirty-five dogs, and for me it was the beginning of a long and wearying saga.

For the time being, this van was her home. In it she had Salukis, Great Danes and Pugs. The chaos in that van is easy to imagine, and Mrs Mountford was in a state approaching nervous collapse. A local vet found her a place to park her van for a few days and offered to board her dogs to give her a rest. A couple of weeks later she left the area, only to return with twenty-nine dogs. She took up residence in a cottage in the hills, and this is where I first came into contact with her.

The place was primitive in the extreme. It was half of an old cottage, with two rooms upstairs and two down. There was no running water, except from a cold tap next door, and no drainage from the stone sink in the kitchen. The only way to drain anything was to collect it in a bowl and throw it into an open gutter which ran along a wall at the back of the building.

The dogs had the run of the house, and used the garden as they pleased. The garden was spattered everywhere with dog-droppings which were never cleared away. The house stank.

Despite the horrors of her surroundings, Mrs Mountford was operating one of the largest of the cottage breeding establishments. She had dogs and bitches among her Pugs, so she could breed from them by herself, and she hired stud dogs to breed from her Saluki and Great Dane bitches. Unfortunately, she was finding it impossible to make ends meet. She was a persuasive woman, and by continual pleading with the milkman and various local tradesmen she had managed to run up bills far in excess of reasonable limits. Then the tradesmen began to foreclose on her and she became increasingly desperate and, so I heard, even suicidal.

Mrs Mountford began to behave as if she was under siege, and refused to talk to anybody. As I approached the cottage with a police sergeant one day, she poked a rifle out of an upstairs window and started firing.

'Hey,' I shouted, 'are you shooting at me?'

'If I'd meant to shoot *at* you,' she replied, 'you'd be dead.'

Sure enough, she knew how to use a rifle. If I'd had more hair on the top of my head, she would have parted it for me.

The sergeant and I had to break in at the back of the cottage. The back door was of the stable type, and we had got the top half open when Mrs Mountford heard us and came running down the stairs. She reached the back door and pushed the barrel of the rifle out at us. Before she could loose off another skull-shaver, I pulled one half of the door on to the rifle and it jerked out of her hands. The sergeant seized the rifle and we entered the house. Immediately, she quietened down.

She was at the end of her tether. She was now at the stage where she needed help for her own mental condition as well as to keep her house and dogs in some kind of running order. Unfortunately, her business affairs had been neglected for too long and she was unable to restore them by herself. There was also the small matter of her conduct with the rifle. She had to be taken into a mental hospital for a complete rest, and sixteen of the dogs had to be put down.

It was sad, and I felt for her. In her more rational moments she appeared to accept that we had no alternative course of action. At other times, however, she was deeply resentful and sent me a string of threatening letters. I am not complaining; that sort of thing goes with my job. The most important point was that this woman had needed help, and it had been our duty to provide it.

AND WHAT ABOUT THE ANIMALS?

In many of the instances I have described, the dogs, bitches and puppies are caused unnecessary suffering because they are inadequately fed and housed in dirty, makeshift accommodation, where they are much more exposed to disease than they would be in well-kept kennels. There is something else, however, which I find particularly disturbing about the puppy-farming business. This has to do with the treatment of the breeding bitches.

At this low-grade end of the business, it is rare to find any but the most glancing consideration paid to the animals which are at the heart of it all: the bitches who give birth to litter after litter of puppies for the breeder to sell. It can be a vicious circle in that poverty drives people to exploit what assets they possess even harder than they would if they were less poor. This is no consolation for the bitches who are seldom allowed to miss a season and so have almost no time to recover from having one litter, raising it and being parted from it, before they are expecting the next litter of puppies.

This misuse of the breeding bitches, who are treated like machines in a factory, is one of the worst aspects of the puppy trade. It is also one of the hardest to put a stop to, because the courts are chiefly concerned with other matters such as feeding and housing and whether the establishment is a health hazard or not. They are not really concerned with the everyday wellbeing of an animal until this has been put severely at risk. Only by persuading and putting pressure on the breeders themselves can we hope to change some of the norms by which the trade currently operates. The treatment of breeding bitches is high on my list of priorities.

In this chapter I have described many unpleasant aspects of the puppy farming business. You have read about diseased puppies, run-down establishments, overworked bitches, the selling of puppies by hire purchase and mail order, and the distressing and sometimes fatal conditions in which puppies are transported across the country.

I would ask one thing: that you remember this little chapter should you ever want to buy a puppy for yourself or your family. As I noted earlier, if everyone bought their puppies direct from reputable licensed breeders, this down-at-heel trade with its dealers and middle-men, its squalor and deprivations would be forced out of existence. It is my real hope that, one day, it will be.

── FROG RACING, AND ──
─OTHER SPORTS REPORTS ─

Sometimes we slip up. We receive a piece of information at our Group HQ and act on it in good faith, but the reality turns out to be far from anything we had imagined.

One of our education officers told me that a group of over-eighteens were planning to hold a frog-racing tournament for charity. She thought we should investigate it and I agreed with her. This was very much the kind of exploitation of animals that we are anxious to prevent.

To several people I spoke to, the idea of a frog race recalled the old childhood trick of sticking a straw under a frog's bottom to make it jump. We did not want that sort of thing to become fashionable again.

We found out that the event was to be held in a pub in a small town near Leeds. To give me some cover, I asked my wife Sue to come along with me. On the night fixed for the frog racing, we went there looking, we hoped, like an average couple out for a quiet evening together. I was wearing civvies. I bought our drinks and we sat in a corner.

After a few minutes we began wondering if we had come to the right place, because it looked very dead. Then a customer came in, ordered his pint, and in a loud voice asked:

'Is it right you're having frog racing here tonight?'

The woman behind the bar said: 'Yes, and I hope they don't leave any about – 'cos I'm scared of 'em.'

'Well, I'm bloody disgusted,' said the bloke. 'I think you ought to tell the RSPCA about this.'

He sat down, and I nodded to Sue. At least we knew we had come to the right place. Soon a few young people came into the bar, and I noticed that some of them were carrying plastic shopping bags which chinked and clanked as they moved. They must have jam jars in there, I thought. They've brought their frogs in jam jars.

After a while these youngsters began to go upstairs. The landlady said to one girl: 'Now, don't you leave any lying about.' The girl laughed at this and walked on up the stairs.

I gave them a few more minutes. No one else came in and I could hear a few bangs and thumps coming through the ceiling. I thought: Right, now's the time to move. I dashed upstairs.

On the landing I quickly located the door to the room where the noise was. I paused for an instant, then gripped the door handle and thrust the door open. A rapid glance round the brightly lit room told me all I wanted to know.

They were having a frog-racing tournament, all right. But the frogs were cardboard ones, worked by an elastic band to make them jump. Many eyes turned towards me as I stood there.

'Sorry, wrong room,' I said, all in a rush, and rapidly pulled the door shut behind me. I collected my wife and we retreated swiftly into the night.

GOLDFISH EATING

This was a genuine case, but we never quite got to the bottom of it. With a colleague I went to a certain pub outside Leeds where, every night, a feller was said to swallow live goldfish.

We could have got the venue wrong, because in that district there are two pubs with similar names. On several occasions we went to the pub that seemed the more likely one, but without success. Finally, after we had been going there on and off for about three weeks, the landlord came over and spread a white cloth on a nearby table. We quietly asked him what he was preparing for.

'Oh,' he said, 'we've got a bit of a do on tonight. Something special.'

This must be it, we thought. We *have* got the right place. We waited. A plate of sliced bread was put on the table, and then a glass of water. Our imaginations began to work overtime as we tried to picture the scene in advance. What did he want all that bread for? How many goldfish did he get through in a night?

A few minutes later a crowd of people came into the bar, and soon after that we realized that we had been completely wasting our time. That evening the pub was acting as a stage in a motoring treasure hunt, and the table was for the feller who checked in the various teams.

We never did find the goldfish man – if he ever existed.

Cock and Quail Fights

Hell hath no fury like a gang of men whose sport is threatened, no matter how illegal that sport may be.

Cockfighting is an ancient form of sport – although I personally would not honour it with that name because to my mind it is one of the most barbaric activities I can imagine. Fortunately, many people agree with me and it has long been outlawed in Britain. That has not stopped certain ruthless people from trying to keep it going.

As you may have read in books or newspaper accounts, cockfighting flourishes in some foreign countries, in backward places such as Haiti where it is very big with the gambling fraternity and correspondingly big sums of money change hands at every meeting. So, too, in Britain it can be as much a business as a so-called sport. There are profits to be made, and organizers who will stop at nothing to keep the money coming in.

It is a hard racket to penetrate, as is the related one of quail-fighting. As far as I know, the two are operated by different sections of the community and there is little or no overlap. For us, the biggest problem is to catch them at it. It is no good just finding someone with a quail in his car. He will say he is going to eat it, and there is nothing illegal about that. It is equally useless to turn up at a venue if the people responsible have just done a bunk through the back door. You have no case until you have caught the organizers in the act.

I know what a quail-fighting ring looks like, and I can tell you how they prepare the cock birds for a contest – mixing whisky in their feed to hype them up, shaping their claws to receive the deadly sharp artificial spurs, varnishing their toes, keeping them for long periods in bags so the birds cannot move their wings while the owners drive them hither and thither by car. I have also seen photographs of fights in progress, but what we need is first-hand evidence – for one of our people actually to *be* there while it is happening.

In some areas the quail fighters are highly organized. They have cars at the ready to take customers to a fight, and they are often able to set up and stage an event at short notice. This of course makes it more difficult for us to pick up a rumour and act on it quickly enough to be effective.

Cockfighting operates on similar lines, and the organizers can be ruthless towards outsiders and people like us who try to get in their way. I was watching a particular place with a colleague one evening, and while I was away from my van someone got to it and fixed the brakes, squashing the pipes that carry the fluid to the front wheels. Not realizing this, I drove away and then, going down a hill, pressed the brake pedal; no response. With dawning horror I felt the van gathering speed and the chap with me, a trainee inspector, began to look seriously alarmed. Fortunately for both of us, I was able to regain control with the gears and the handbrake. We found a garage, dumped the van and rang for someone to come and fetch us.

It isn't often that the people we confront get physical. But when they do. . . .

Fox-Hunting – The Pagans and the Posers

I have noticed over the years that, among the so-called cruel sports, those that are banned by law are usually the traditional poor man's sports such as dog-fighting and cock-fighting. I am not saying for a moment that these should not be banned, but equally I do not follow the logic of a legal system which allows a no less cruel sport, such as fox-hunting, to continue.

It tempts me to believe that the future of fox-hunting does not depend on logic at all; what keeps it going is an alliance of reactionary money and power in high places. The same may also be said of game shooting.

As soon as I start to debate the fox-hunting issue with its supporters, someone always brings up the need-to-cull argument. I appreciate that foxes can do a lot of damage to farm property and livestock, and it may sometimes be necessary to reduce the number of foxes in a particular area, but it is not necessary to hunt them down with a pack of dogs whose ambition is to rip their quarry to pieces.

When I was in West Wales some farmers were having a lot of trouble with foxes. Their method of dealing with the problem was to organize a proper limited cull. On the appointed day they went out together and shot a certain number of foxes. The killing was done as cleanly as they could manage, and to my mind those farmers achieved their aim and caused a minimum of suffering to the animals.

Whether it is right that they should be allowed to shoot foxes is another matter. That is a moral issue, and in my work I have to be concerned primarily with practical matters. The first distinction I would make is to say that the farmers' action was surely a whole lot better than setting a pack of dogs on to each individual fox and tearing it apart. Better, too, than the barbaric ritual of smearing a young boy with the fox's blood. That to me is not just pagan or uncivilized, it is wrong. I cannot understand how people allow that to happen to members of their own family.

I am not against those jolly amateurs who like to dress up and go for a ride. Several hunt officials have told me, on the side, that their members only go hunting for the show. They put on the smart clothes, ride to the meet, have a drink . . . and then they are ready to go home again! Often they do just that. They would not know what to do if they saw a fox, and they hope they never will.

Their dogs are equally out of condition. After one of these 'jolly' hunts I was called in to assist the police with a 'huge vicious dog' that was said to be in the yard of a house in a village and would not let anybody near it. I went along there to find that the police sergeant in charge had put himself on point duty up the road, out of the way, leaving me with a constable and a traffic warden. I went into the yard and the 'huge vicious dog' ambled towards me. He was an ancient foxhound as soft as anything and with hardly a tooth left in his head. He might have given you a hard suck, but that was about all. He had certainly come from the hunt, and had either lost his way or decided to take a quiet breather and let the others go on ahead.

Hunters of that calibre – man *and* dog – are no problem. The difficulties arise with the keen so-and-sos, the ones who think there is no finer sport than chasing a fox on horseback across open country with a pack of hounds. That sort of scene may look all right on table mats, but to me it should only be preserved as part of our national heritage if the hunters are prepared to forgo the fox and make do with pursuing a scent trail which someone could draw for them shortly before the meet. In this day and age, most people are prepared to show a decent respect for *all* animals. Why make an exception of the fox?

— BLUEBELL, AND OTHER —
——— CLIFFHANGERS ———

A surprisingly large amount of my time in Wales was spent rescuing farm animals which somehow fell over cliffs and, in Bluebell's case, went for a swim in the bay.

It was the 29th December, and an appropriately cold and windy day, when I received the call. A cow (her nickname was a later invention) had gone into the sea at high tide and had been swept round the rocks. The good news for this 8½ cwt (432 kg) cross-Hereford was that the tide had then pushed her inshore and she had been able to scrabble and force her way into a cave above the high-water mark.

The owner, a Mr Morgan, had contacted the RSPCA. At that time I had a team of air cadets who were willing to help with rescues; most of them could swim and they were all enthusiastic to learn as they went along.

A brief survey from the clifftop told me that there was no way of bringing the cow to safety except by swimming her out to sea from the cave, past two headlands, and then up on to a strip of beach. We prepared to carry out this plan, and were ready for action when a local expert (self-appointed) suggested very firmly that we should wait until the tide went out; then we would find it much easier to get down to the cow, he said. We waited, but it was a complete waste of time. That day a backing wind was blowing and the tide did not go out. A helicopter was available for the rescue, and we considered using it to try to winch the cow to safety. Probably this would have worked in reasonable weather conditions, but the high wind was against us; the helicopter could not get in close enough to the cliff, and we abandoned this method.

There was nothing for it but for two of us to climb down to the cow by rope, make her secure and then plunge with her into the cold, cold waves and hope to swim her round the headlands. Down I clambered with a cadet flight-sergeant called Anthony Morgan. After briefly trying to comfort the discomforted cow (I think it was about now that she became 'Bluebell'), we got her tethered to secondary ropes. These were held by a team working with considerable difficulty on the very slippery rocks of the cliff. They were our only back-up should anything go wrong with the next phase of the operation, in which Sid Jenkins, Tony Morgan and Bluebell took to the icy-cold waters.

Cows *can* swim. That was not our main problem. Once we had contrived, with help, to lever Bluebell over the lip of the cave entrance and into the sea, she adapted to her new surroundings and set about steadily powering her bulk in a westerly direction across Cardigan Bay. She was quicker than I had thought possible, and our main problem was to deflect her from swimming towards a distant point on the Irish coast, somewhere in County Wicklow or thereabouts, and guide her back to Wales.

I would not like to say how long we were in the water. My report, written shortly after the adventure, notes that the cow and her escorts did succeed in rounding the two headlands and in due course, 'after some difficulty in finding a footing, the animal was brought ashore at Aberporth beach where she was rubbed down, covered with sacks and taken to a farm'.

For my part, I was neither rubbed down nor covered with sacks, but do remember getting to the farmhouse where a bottle of something lovely and warming was produced, and the farmer's wife laid on a meal for the whole rescue squad.

Bluebell became quite a local celebrity after that. In fact, I don't think she ever went off to market – just dined out on her great escapade, I imagine, posing eternally for the cameras of the local newspapers.

NOT EVEN A CUP OF TEA

The press in Wales became quite keen on our animal rescues, and it was not long before a local reporter called Graham Jenkins attached himself to our team. His intention was to go with us on a rescue and write it up afterwards. To his surprise, he found himself roped in (literally) to help: he even ended up with a Certificate of Merit from the RSPCA.

On this occasion a ewe had got herself trapped on a ledge over some cliffs above a river. My usual call for volunteers produced three policemen – an inspector, a sergeant and a constable – and the reporter from the local newspaper. Together we drove off to the scene of the emergency, which was near a village in the hills, about twenty-five miles inland from the sea.

I had worked in this area before, and well knew that it had its natural drawbacks (as well as a human one that we will come to later). Not only were the cliffs steep and difficult, there were no nearby roads and so to reach the site a rescue squad had to hump all our rescue gear up a narrow track for two and a half miles.

When we reached the clifftop we were able to locate the animal without difficulty. The cliff itself did not just consist of one perpendicular wall, there was also a very steep path running down it, and what the ewe had done was to stray from this path. Perhaps she had slipped, and in her scrambling efforts to save herself had landed on a narrow ledge of rock from which she was then unable to move. My task would be to go down to her on a rope and somehow swing her sideways off the ledge and on to the path. Once she had her hooves on the path again, I was confident that she would be able to make her own way to safety.

I was lowered slowly towards the ewe. The surface of the rock was uneven and, in some places, crumbling. Pieces were shaken loose by my descent, some of them whistling past my nose and the odd one or two cracking me on the head before hurtling all the way to the bottom of the gorge some three or four hundred feet below.

Nor was it all beer and skittles for my helpers. They had anchored my rope, and themselves, to the only suitable rock on that part of the cliff and it was no easy task to lower and raise me from that position. They also had the additional burden of my safety to worry about.

They stuck to their task, and eventually I was able to reach the ewe and move it to safety. Then I was hauled back to the top of the cliff. It had been a long operation, lasting three and a half hours, and at the end of it I was tired and thirsty. I began to long for a strong cup of tea. No chance, of course, I quickly reminded myself. As far as cups of tea were concerned, we were on the wrong farm. This farmer did not even thank people for rescuing his animals.

I knew him from a previous rescue. Some while previously I had been involved in a bigger operation which had included both the police and the fire brigade. When it was over, the police were the first to go, followed by the firemen. I was left standing in a

Left: Freddy, the nearly toothless fox. Eating from the city's dustbins, his junk-food diet had taken its toll on his molars.

Photo: *Yorkshire Evening Post*

Below: Peter the fox in the compound at the RSPCA's Wildlife Unit in Somerset, before being released to begin a natural life again.

Blackie was a victim of complete neglect. Kept indoors, unwanted and unloved, he was riddled with fleas when found by the RSPCA. Seen here before treatment, his coat falling away if touched, he was a pitiful sight.

After receiving much care and attention from the staff at Leeds
RSPCA Animal Home, Blackie is a happy and healthy dog again.
He is introduced by me to his new owner, Alf Taylor, and prepares
to travel to his new home.

Photo: *The Star*

When Knaresborough Zoo
had to close at short notice,
calamity faced its almost 300
animals. This lucky young
bear, called Precious, found a
new home. Her parents were
not so fortunate.

Roma, the Sumatran tigress,
was another at
Knaresborough Zoo to escape
death. She joined Kaffa, the
black leopard, in a new home
at Linton Zoo, and was
adopted by 74 (Tiger)
Squadron RAF based at
Stowmarket, Suffolk.

Catch that cockerel! This cock – suspected of having been used in cockfighting – was abandoned in a derelict factory compound. Trainee inspector Paul Stilgo was given the awkward job of catching the bird.

Photo: *Sunday Mirror*

This poster was the winner in a competition I ran every year while writing pet care articles for the *Yorkshire Evening Post*. It was produced by a pupil of the City of Leeds School and showed the perils of fireworks on Guy Fawkes' night.

This pit has been used for
animal baiting. A little later,
I discovered garments that
were, I was told by witches,
used in rituals involving
animals.

Photo: *Yorkshire Evening Post*

No animal is entirely safe at
all times. This sandwich had
been poisoned and put down
to kill off birds and cats by
someone with a grudge.
Photo: *Yorkshire Evening Post*

Above: A pack of stray dogs, one of many that roam the streets of Leeds or any big city.

Photo: *Yorkshire Evening Post*

Right: With staff from Bradford Animal Home, I survey the site which will provide more kennels for dogs, a landscaped area for wildlife and accommodation for all types of animals. Interested inmates look on!

Photo: *Yorkshire Evening Post*

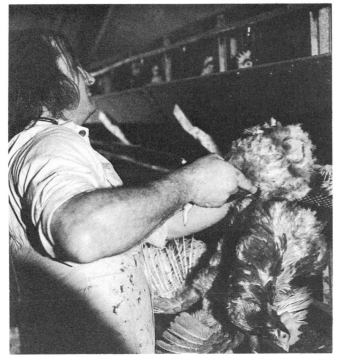

Above: One of the most dramatic BBC TV *Animal Squad* programmes featured this ramshackle battery chicken unit. Live chickens laid eggs on top of the bodies of dead ones. Only dead chickens were found in this derelict building. The owners were successfully prosecuted.

Left: Chicken farmer removes live birds from battery cages, to send them for slaughter.
Photo: *Paul Berriff*

A swan that had been trapped
in a coal mine, about to be
cleaned up before being
released into the wild.

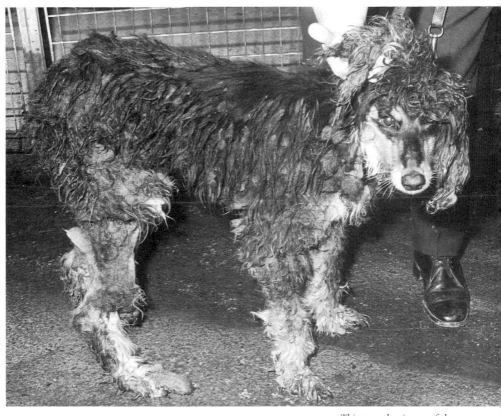

This poor dog is one of three
Afghan hounds found
neglected that I brought into
Leeds Animal Home. The
owners were convicted of
causing unnecessary suffering,
fined and disqualified from
keeping a dog.

The Rabbit Game. I and a
uniformed colleague,
Inspector Kevin Manning,
confront the driver of the
rabbits and tackle him about
the poor state of the crates in
which rabbits were to have
been carried on their journey
to slaughter.
Photo: *Paul Berriff*

Responding – on call sign 'Lima One' – to a call from the Group
Communications Centre. There is an RSPCA Inspector available 24
hours a day in every region of England and Wales.

Photo: *The Star*

Orlando ('Landy' for short) is my friend, companion and a Double
Supreme Premier Cat of the Cat Association of Great Britain.
Found abandoned in a box with other kittens, he has returned the
kindness time and time again. A TV star in his own right, Landy
has a cartoon strip and story featuring him every week in the Junior
Post section of the *Yorkshire Evening Post*.

Photo: *Woman Magazine*

field, collecting up my equipment, when I saw the farmer coming towards me. Oh, I thought, he's going to ask me to thank the others when I see them.

The farmer stopped about ten yards from me and pointed, then uttered his benediction. 'If you're last out,' he called, 'shut the gate.'

FIREMAN'S LIFT

A bullock had gone over a cliff and the farmer (not Mr 'Shut-Gate') had called the fire brigade. The firemen were a part-time outfit, drawn from several nearby villages, and before I reached the scene all they had managed to do was to drop the bullock even further down the cliff.

In charge of the part-timers was a Divisional Fire Officer – a Very Important Person, or so he clearly thought. He was determined to show his 'men' how the job should be done. Next thing, he was lowered over the cliff on a rope, and shortly after that he got himself well and truly stuck on a narrow piece of ledge. In my RSPCA uniform I was quickly deemed the next person most likely to succeed, and it fell to me to go down the cliff and rescue the rescuer.

When I reached him it was obvious that he was stuck because he had seized up with fright, and in that condition could move neither one way nor the other. Despite his terror, he was still able to feel equally horrified by something else – the damage being done to his reputation as his juniors leaned over the cliff top and marvelled at the mess he had got himself into.

'Get me off this bloody ledge,' he muttered to me as I arrived beside him. 'My God, I've never felt such a fool!'

He all but banged his head against the cliff, so intense was his frustration. After a bit of a struggle I managed to move him sideways on my rope and got him on to a broader ledge. There, at least, he could feel reasonably safe. I was in no hurry to have him raised to the top of the cliff, where he was quite capable of fouling up some other part of the job in hand. We still had the bullock to rescue, and I wanted to get that done as soon as possible, without further interference.

To protect what was left of the Divisional Officer's self-esteem, I told him that I was going down the cliff for the bullock and I would like him to remain in the middle, where he was, and give orders to the people at the top.

This was a real face-saver for him, and he agreed. Off I went, leaving him to yell orders to his waiting juniors. When I had completed the rescue, I returned to the cliff top and the Divisional Officer was hauled up to join the rest of us. Whether his juniors were impressed by his performance was difficult to tell; they gave no sign of their feelings beyond the occasional twitch – or were they trying not to laugh?

DING DONG BELL

A lamb fell down a mineshaft on 1st April, and I set off into the hills with three policemen who had volunteered to help me. For some rescues we use a canvas bag which is put round the animal to control its movements; this also makes it easier for us to raise and lower it by rope. I had one of these bags with me when the policemen lowered me into the mineshaft.

It was dark in there, but not so dark that I couldn't see the bottom. Down and down I went, until with a jerk I stopped. Not, unfortunately, with my feet on the floor of the shaft; the rope was a little bit too short, and I had to untie myself from it and jump the rest of the way.

I located the lamb and pressed it to me to give it some warmth. I picked it up and turned towards the rope, reaching upwards. No good; it was too high for me.

I called up the mineshaft: 'Put some spare rope on the end, will you. I can't reach this.'

From the top of the shaft I heard some spluttering and laughter, then a voice called back to me: 'We haven't brought any of the spare rope with us. We'll have to go back and fetch it.'

'What do you mean?' I shouted. 'You must have some more rope.'

More mysterious laughter, then: 'No. No, we haven't. We'll just fetch it now. You stay there.'

There followed a small hoot of triumph from up top, then I heard them moving away. That's good, I thought, they *are* leaving me. 'You stay there,' they had said. Very funny. Where else do they expect me to go, I'm not Spiderman.

But what was so funny about it? I asked myself, settling back with the lamb and resigning myself to a long wait. Why all the laughter? I still couldn't make it out.

Ah! I know! April Fool's Day, that's why! The thought came to me at last, and I acknowledged it with a wry smile. My colleagues the policemen had wanted to play a little joke on their colleague the animal bloke. So they had pushed off to the village pub for a quick bevvy and a good laugh at my expense.

At twelve o'clock the joke came to an end when the policemen returned. The rope – which in reality had not been run out to its full length – was extended down to me. The lamb and I were hauled up to the daylight, and to the less enchanting spectacle of three guffawing policemen.

YOUR LIFE NOT IN THEIR HANDS

At the beginning of this next rescue we had the Fire Brigade to help us. Then, just as we reached the site, they received a call out to a fire and had to go off, leaving me with a handful of volunteers.

On this occasion it was a prize ram which had strayed too close to the cliff edge and gone over. I am not saying that this ram was more important in my eyes than other rams just because he had won a few prizes; that would not be true. However, the farmer was obviously quite excited, and very keen to get him back.

The ram had slipped a long way down and then been stopped on a ledge. In charge of the ropes, and the belaying operation at the top of the cliff, was a police officer. He was holding my rope as I was lowered down the cliff in the usual way. Everything at that stage was going as it should except that the wind was gusting furiously and making a lot of noise.

As I picked my way down the cliff, I suddenly felt the rope go slack. I knew this should not have happened; the rope should remain taut all the way through the climb – all the way down and all the way back. It puzzled me, but there was little I could do about it because the wind was howling so much that I had no chance of being heard up top, however loudly I shouted. I carried on, creeping very slowly down the rock and making sure I had secure holds before I made each move. Now the rope was really sagging; I had about a foot of slack. What was going on? Why didn't they take it up?

Then I was close to the ledge where the ram waited. He watched me approach with some trepidation, but his fears were not shared by me; I just wanted to get my feet securely on that ledge, whatever the ram thought about it. As I did so, the line went taut again.

The rescue was completed with no further problems. I made the ram fast and gave the signal and he was hauled up to safety. Then I followed, clambering back up my line until I reached the cliff top. I swung a leg over on to the flat grass, and there stood the police officer, watching me.

'What are you doing there?' I asked him. 'I thought you were holding me.'

'Oh, no,' he said, 'I went for a pee behind that bush.' He pointed, as if showing me which bush would explain everything.

I said: 'So, who was holding the rope?'

'Nobody,' he replied, his eyes growing wider as comprehension dawned. 'I thought it was dug into the ground.'

It most certainly was not dug into the ground. The rope, attached to its metal stake, had pulled out. That was when it had gone slack on me the first time. Then the rope, anchored to nothing, began to slither towards the edge of the cliff. Luckily for me, it then came to a stop where I eventually found it – caught in the base of a tractor wheel.

By chance the farmer had parked his tractor near the cliff top, and the wheel had served as a grappling point, supporting me for the remainder of my climb. If it had not done so, there would have been nothing else between there and the cliff. . . .

From that day I made it one of the guiding principles of my life – my second life, you might say, since I had just forfeited the first through carelessness: NEVER, EVER go down a cliff until you have seen that your rope has been made fast. I have followed that principle ever since, and it has kept me out of further trouble.

Rescues have become much more tightly organized since those rough-and-ready days in the Seventies. We now have specialists in each RSPCA region who deal with particularly dangerous situations. There is a climbing expert, for instance, a water expert, and so on. If I did today some of the things I did then, the Health and Safety people would be after me and I would be soundly told off for taking unnecessary risks. Quite right, too.

DOGS FOR SECURITY

Some of our housing estates have been getting into a terrible state of decay. Since the economic recession made itself felt in the community, around 1980, money has been very much tighter; repairs that once would have been thought essential are no longer treated as such, and many are ignored altogether. Broken windows are not replaced; instead the spaces are filled in with pieces of board. Some of our streets look as if they have been through a battle or a siege, although in fact no battle or siege has taken place.

Those eyeless windows are part of a longer process. The decline in people's living standards has brought other changes: thefts are up, and many neighbours do not trust each other. They have become unreasonably frightened of further thefts, whether of household goods or the contents of the gas or electricity meter. As a deterrent, they have been getting themselves a dog.

Animals like this are not to be confused with pets; they are there to do the job of a burglar alarm. They are tied up at the back of the garden and encouraged to bark if anyone comes. They are deprived of company and affection; the owners do not see affection as a necessary part of the deal. They didn't pay all that money for a hearthrug; besides, they think, the dog would go soft if they made a fuss of it.

This is bad for the dog, for several reasons. Dogs are pack animals and thrive on company. When we take a dog into our home we assume the position of head of the pack in the dog's eyes. The owner is the one the dog wants to look up to and learn from. If it is starved of company, it becomes bored and this affects its temperament. If people must keep a dog in order to protect the contents of their home – a motive I deplore – then I would at least suggest that the dog would be better employed behind the doors of the house rather than tied up in the garden. Someone intending to break in could simply ignore a tied-up dog and rob the house anyway.

Getting a guard dog is for some people a bit like joining the arms race. They feel they must have a tough dog with a reputation for this kind of work. They think about it for a couple of days, and decide that only a Geman Shepherd will do. Or perhaps a

Dobermann. These and Dobermann-crosses are becoming quite popular at the moment. Unfortunately, such dogs cost a lot of money to buy and feed properly. I have seen too many thin, badly undernourished guard dogs to doubt that there are a lot of owners who panic themselves into getting a dog without giving serious thought to how they are going to look after it.

The whole business is both sad and a very poor reflection on the kind of society we have created for ourselves. Until there is widespread social change, which I think must include better housing for many people, as well as a better general environment, then I am afraid the future is looking bleak. So far as the use of dogs is concerned, we have taken 'man's best friend' and begun turning him into our enemy. That is a desperate thing to have happened.

On a commercial level, guard dogs are big business. Security firms use them to guard all kinds of buildings and yards. Many dogs are left out all night, tied up. This is wrong; a guard dog should always be under the control of a handler. All the same, it happens.

We now have a Guard Dogs Act, which came into being in 1975, but only one section of it has been implemented, which leaves a lot of loopholes. Meanwhile a lucrative trade has sprung up selling guard dogs abroad, to nations such as Nigeria. In my view this trade needs very careful monitoring. Although it is not in itself illegal it involves some very undesirable practices. For example, a consignment of dogs will be crated up and flown out to Africa when the supplier knows full well that most of the dogs will not last longer than six months at their destination. The heat gets to them. They can't do the job expected of them because they are exhausted. A few weeks of that and the owner can't wait to be rid of them – if they haven't already become hopelessly weak and died.

Given that there is a market for guard dogs in these hot countries, it beats me why the governments there don't encourage breeding establishments to be set up to raise dogs locally. It would be a great deal cheaper than importing them from Britain – a recent consignment of twenty dogs sent to Nigeria cost the buyer £12,000 – and locally bred dogs would be able to cope so much better with the climate and conditions.

The development of this trade is something we must all

watch out for. It is an insidious, creeping practice, and it begins under our very noses. Advertisements appear in the newspapers which say: 'WANTED. Dogs to be trained as Guard Dogs. Write, etc.' This kind of advertisement is calculated to catch the eye of someone with a dog they cannot afford to keep. To them it seems like a godsend: they will actually be paid (though not much) to have the dog taken off their hands at a time when it has become an increasing liability and they have felt depressingly stuck with it. Short of driving it somewhere and dumping it, they have run out of ideas about what to do next – when all of a sudden this advertisement appears.

To anyone in this position, I would like to add the following thought. All right, if you do a deal with the Guard Dog people, the dog will be off your hands and you won't have to worry about being able to feed and look after it. But please also bear in mind that you may be sending your dog to spend the rest of its life in misery, chained up in some yard where the unbearable heat, flies and disease will quickly bring it down and it will die. Surely it would be better to take the dog to the RSPCA or to another suitable animal charity, where it can hope to find new owners who will give it a caring home, or even to have it humanely destroyed by a qualified person rather than have to face a six-month death sentence in the heat of West Africa.

THE TIN MINE
CAT WIDOW

Just occasionally my role is reversed, and instead of rescuing the animal I have to go in and save the owner. The case of the Tin Mine Cat Widow still stands out in my memory.

Mrs Morgan, as we will call her, lived by herself in an old and tumbling-down cottage near a disused tin mine in West Wales, about ten miles from the coast. We first heard about her through the local milkman, who had been puzzled when, for no apparent reason, her milk order went up from three pints to six. Then it went up to nine. Next thing, someone had boarded up the windows of the cottage and blocked the glass panel in the door. The milk order had remained at nine pints, but now it was impossible to see into the house; most mysterious, what was going on? Cats were in evidence around the place, but how many there were, no one knew. Perhaps there were other, larger animals, but again no one knew. I decided we had to get in there and see for ourselves.

The scene we found was so weird, we needed several minutes to take it all in. The cottage had become a kind of mad prison, in which a band of unruly cats were effectively holding poor Mrs Morgan in helpless captivity.

Cats were everywhere. On the furniture, on the floor amid smashed crockery, up the curtains, everywhere. On a chest of drawers stood a swivelling mirror. When we arrived, a cat was crouched beside the mirror, batting it with one paw so that it swung sharply through the air, first one way, then the other. Each time the mirror slowed down, the cat gave it another smack and off it went again. A haunting sight – like something in a horror movie.

The cats, truly, had taken over. The smell was terrible, and there was little that had not been damaged – the curtains sagging and torn, the upholstery ripped, the paintwork scratched and smeared. . . But what of Mrs Morgan herself?

She sat in her chair in the middle of it all, alone and terrified, her arms and legs stiff and unmoving, as though glued in position. It seemed, from the state of her, that she must have taken root in the chair several days previously. All round her the feline terror had raged, and she had grown increasingly unable either to resist, influence or do anything about it.

I had seen enough. 'All right,' I said to Mrs Morgan, 'we'll sort this out for you.'

Without waiting for a reply – and I don't think she was offering one – we went to work collecting up the cats and taking them away. There was no alternative: some of them were half-wild and in poor health, and, anyway, they were the villains of the piece, the obvious source of Mrs Morgan's distress. They had to be moved out.

Getting hold of them was another matter. When a semi-starving, very disorderly cat is clinging to the top of a curtain, its first instinct when you approach is not to leap softly into your arms and start purring. If you try and reach up to it with your bare hands, it will claw you to bits.

To cope with this problem we have a special implement which is known as a 'grasper'. This is a long metal tube with a length of cord running through it which forms a loop at the far, or business, end. The idea is to manoeuvre the loop over the animal's head and catch it by the neck. Once its movements are limited in this way, you have a much better chance of getting in close. From there you can lower the animal into a basket and the job is neatly and quickly done.

Even with the grasper's assistance, we were a long time clearing those cats out of Mrs Morgan's cottage. We counted them out and the total came to thirty-seven! In the meantime we had arranged for Mrs Morgan to be taken to hospital to recover from her strange and frightening experience. When she left, I still did not really know what had been going on in her house. Only later, when she emerged from the shock of it all, did we hear the full story.

Mrs Morgan's troubles began when she took in two cats, a male and a female who were also brother and sister. In time the female produced kittens, but this did not please Mrs Morgan at all. In fact she was horrified. A deeply religious woman, she believed that this was against God's will. Brother and sister should not mate; she felt ashamed. Her next reaction was fear: not for the future of the cats, but fear that any of her neighbours should find out what had happened, and blame her for it. She could not bear the thought of becoming a target for gossip and pointing fingers. She decided she should keep herself to herself. She increased the daily milk order by three pints, so the cats and kittens would not lack for basic nourishment, but to the outside world it was almost as though she had disappeared.

The weeks went by, months went by, the kittens matured into cats and, as was bound to happen, the young females came into season for the first time and were mated. More kittens arrived, and soon the cottage was overrun by a feline horde whose members did what they pleased, there being no one to control them. Mrs Morgan could feel nothing but mounting shame and desperation; the longer it went on, the worse it became. She barricaded the windows and the front door and fell into a kind of mental and physical stupor. In the last phase before we found her she had taken to sitting in her armchair for so long, while the cats roamed and fought around her, that the hours had dissolved into days and she scarcely knew what was happening. She had broken down.

Most of the cats had to be destroyed. Interbred, half-wild and in poor condition, they had little future to speak of.

Luckily, Mrs Morgan was not seriously affected by her ordeal. When she came out of hospital, she was bright and well and had recovered her optimism. We gave her two cats, a male and a female which had been neutered and spayed, and she settled down to a new, peaceful life.

Her story had a happy ending – but only just. It was the nearest episode, in my experience, to those cinema films where the animals take over a human community. Alfred Hitchcock's *The Birds* is a good example. You think, don't you, that it could never happen in real life. . . .

— FEUDING ON THE FARM —

This is the story of a long and extraordinary case in which the chief performers were a family of feuding Welsh hill farmers. I shall not attempt to burden you with every twist and turn in the action, but for me it was an important case because it showed what can happen all too easily when people become so obsessed with their own lives and relationships that they forget their responsibilities to others. In this instance, it was the farm animals which suffered most.

In the beginning, or as far back in time as we need to go, there were three of them. Two brothers and a sister. We will call them the Prices. John Price, Mervyn Price and Megan Price. Since the death of their parents they ran two neighbouring farms – or in theory they did. The trouble with the Prices was that they did not get on together. To be more precise, they hated each other. Maybe there were other things they hated, like being stuck for their entire lives with looking after a piece of remote Welsh hillside. In fact, Megan had already declared her hatred of farming by moving away to a town further south. This, however, did not remove the huge barrier of frustration and bitterness between them, and the only way they were able to deal with it was by endlessly fighting each other. On one occasion, I heard, the two brothers had been seen throwing lime at each other.

Most of the time the feuding took place in a series of two-against-one alliances. John and Megan versus Mervyn. Mervyn and Megan versus John. Always the sister with one of the brothers; never by herself. Perhaps this was what ensured the continuity of the arrangement. As long as the sister had an ally, they all felt safe. Perhaps the thing they feared most of all was that something would one day happen to break up their strange triangle. It may have been hell to live in, but at least they understood the moves.

Well, by the time I came to know the Prices, something had happened. Mervyn had fallen ill and died. That, of course, had left John and Megan. Or, rather, John versus Megan. An unfamiliar battle order in which both of them occupied equally isolated positions and felt even less able to cope with their daily lives and the needs of the two family farms. The surviving brother and sister were both in their early sixties and looked set to carry this private war to their graves.

The two farms stood side by side on top of a hill. Before Mervyn's death John, the eldest, had owned one farm entirely; the other was divided between the three of them. If that brought problems enough, they were as nothing compared to the situation that then arose out of the terms of Mervyn's will. For, instead of leaving his one-third share equally to his brother and sister, so that they then owned the farm on a fifty-fifty basis, he had left his entire share to Megan, his sister. This new, uneven system of ownership provoked a fresh wave of violent rows between John and Megan Price. He loathed the idea of putting any money into an establishment in which his sister was the senior partner, and they argued endlessly about who should pay the bills or what each should contribute towards paying them. Megan also accused John, rightly it seems, of snatching back some of the feed destined for the shared farm and using it to feed the animals on his own land.

I was called on the scene because one day John Price took the quarrel a stage further than it had ever gone before. He drove into town, walked into the local police station and announced that he and his men had withdrawn their labour from both farms. From that day there would be no milking or feeding done by them.

Later that day I telephoned Megan Price and told her what had happened. She immediately said that there was nothing she could do to help. She sounded quite adamant and I sensed at the time that I had just wandered on to a minefield. I rang her accountant and asked him if he could persuade Miss Price to go with him to the farms to inspect them; I would be there as well, and would have a policeman with me.

The accountant also met with a firm refusal. She was not prepared to go to either of the farms and risk confrontation with her brother. Whatever face-to-face rows they might have had in the past, they were no longer on speaking terms. Later that evening, accompanied by a vet and a police officer, I went and inspected the farms. I found that both contained dairy cows. At John Price's own farm the cows had been milked and there was milk in the bulk tank in the dairy; the yearlings, however, were hungry and noisy and it was fairly obvious that they had not been fed. On the shared farm the bulk tank was empty. I asked the vet to check the cows and he reported that there were no signs of suffering; the likely explanation was that they had been milked and the bulk tank emptied. To that extent, John Price had apparently been pulling the wool over our eyes. However, the housed yearlings were clearly hungry and making a lot of noise, and we were unable to locate any foodstuff on the premises. John Price was nowhere to be seen. We went home.

The following evening, at around 6.30, I was driving back to the farm when I came across a stray heifer in the road. I turned it into the farmyard which was nearby, and then found John Price. I told him of my concern for the housed yearlings which were not being fed. Then, in line with our normal procedure, I cautioned him about not having to say anything but, if he did, it might be taken down and used in evidence against him. He decided that he nevertheless wanted to make a statement.

He told me that milking on the shared farm had ceased because his men had withdrawn their labour. (This was not strictly true; as I later found out, he had ordered them to do so, which is hardly the same thing.)

'Before these animals die,' he went on, 'I wish to make it clear that I am not responsible for this state of affairs. Last week I sent advance notice of the men's action to my sister. Four men are involved, and I don't know whether they will return to work next week. I don't expect them to. I will throw the animals a bit of straw in the meantime, but I can't cut silage because of my back.'

He also told me that there was a boy on his own farm who had carried on working because his conscience would not let him stop. He added that he was very worried about the state things had reached on the two farms. He was prepared to meet his sister and her advisers to discuss their problems and he would travel anywhere necessary to do this.

I replied that I was not at all happy with the way things were going. Animals were not being fed and were getting out on the road. I warned him that I was going to report him, then I left.

Next day, again with the vet, I returned at midday. John Price was there and I told him I was planning to go and visit his sister to try and arrange a meeting. He said he would be grateful if I would do this. We then went to inspect some of the outlying animals. In a shed I found some twenty-four yearlings who were now looking in poor condition. They were hungry and their bellies had none of the barrel shape that you expect to find in healthy cattle.

'Look at this,' I said to him. 'You can't just let them get worse.'

'I know it's bad,' he replied, 'but what can I do with this daft sister of mine.'

I told him that he must make more of an effort to feed his animals and keep the farm in proper running order until his differences with his sister were sorted out.

While I was there I also found that a yearling heifer had fallen into the slurry pit. It was the same animal that I had found loose in the road the previous evening. I had pointed this out at the time to the farmer and he had promised to take care of it properly, but obviously he hadn't. We pulled it out of the slurry, and the vet checked it over to make sure it was not damaged, then we went up to the other farm to make a further check on the animals there.

We counted forty-two outliers and they all seemed to be in good condition. From just this brief survey it was clear that John Price was looking after the animals on his own farm but neglecting those on the farm he shared with his sister.

That evening I drove to the sister's house, a journey of some 40 miles, and emphasized that her cattle were deteriorating. If she did not want to end up in court, she would have to take real steps to make sure they were fed and cared for.

'All right, Mr Jenkins,' she said at length. 'I will agree to pay for the cattle on my farm to be fed. But *he* [the unmentionable brother] has got to agree to sell some of the animals to pay for it. I have no money available here, but I will sign a company cheque if he sends it to me with a copy of the bill.

'No,' she went on, sensing that I was about to make a suggestion, 'I can't come to the farm myself because *he* is there. If he wasn't, if he went away for a while, and I knew I would not meet him, I would be able to take a more direct interest. But that is all I can do for now.'

It was something, I thought. It was an offer to feed the animals. All the same, I could not let it rest there. Even if the two of them managed to co-operate to the extent of buying one or possibly two loads of feed, I had no confidence at all in their ability to keep up the arrangement for any length of time. In a week or two, the animals would be neglected again; John Price would send his men out, and we would be back where we started.

Over the next couple of weeks I tried everything to bring the brother and sister together and sort out the dispute once and for all. Meetings were fixed, then cancelled because one pulled out, or failed to turn up. It was hopeless and I had to resort to the law. We took John Price to court, charged with causing unnecessary suffering to an animal. He conducted his own defence in a most long-winded manner, but we secured the conviction – a fine of £25 plus costs for a similar amount.

The court action served the useful purpose of bringing the goings-on at the two farms to the attention of the authorities, but it also had the negative effect of upsetting John Price still more and he began to act as if the whole world was against him.

He withdrew his labour for a second time, and now I felt that we had to make a much more forceful intervention. This did not please me greatly because it meant that I had to take on the additional role of Jenkins the Farmer. I had to buy in straw and food and arrange for the cows to be milked. It was a large herd, bigger than I had ever handled before, and although we brought in a man who was used to milking by machine we often had to do it by hand because Mr Price was not prepared to pay the cost of the electricity and cut the power off. This was in the middle of winter, with snow on the ground, and I can tell you that you needed to be devoted to milking cows to get any fun out of dealing with that lot twice a day!

Mr Price, meanwhile, was living in solitary squalor in a garage on the farm. Primitive is not an adequate word to describe that man's domestic arrangements. The first time I was able to get him to speak to me, I had to break into the garage. I found him naked except for a vest – a not very clean vest, I could add – and all around him on the floor were tins of Main Course soup. As far as I could see it was his only source of food. Clearly, he had let himself go in a fairly serious way; he was badly depressed and rarely showed himself voluntarily on either farm while we were there.

It was all very sad that this should have happened. However, from my point of view it was more than a family feud. A large number of animals were innocently caught in the middle of it all, and a proper lasting solution had to be found and somehow enforced.

Whilst all this was going on, I started a second court case. This was treated as an emergency. A special court was convened, at which both brother and sister were charged with causing unnecessary suffering. The court sat all day, from 10.30 a.m. until well after 6 p.m., and at no time during all this did Mr and Miss Price speak one word to each other. In the end the sister was found not guilty as charged but the bench expressed its concern at what was happening and urged her to sort matters out with her brother in a satisfactory way.

John Price was found guilty and fined £30 on each of two charges plus costs of £250. The chairman of the bench said that they had considered the possibility of banning him from keeping animals but had decided not to impose a ban on this occasion.

Again the court had not been particularly decisive, and predictably the affair dragged on into another round of disputes, neglected animals, and countless proddings from me which went largely unheeded. There was another court case, further convictions, and round we went again. Mr Price then made an offer of £32,000 to try and buy out his sister's two-thirds share. She was unwilling to proceed until a proper valuation was done, and it then emerged that there would be problems with capital gains tax and with gift tax. It all looked insoluble and, once more, the animals on the farm were beginning to suffer.

Finally, in a desperate attempt to knock the whole protracted business on the head, we took the pair of them to court and laid fourteen charges against them. On the day itself we withdrew seven of the charges and John Price's case was heard first. He was cleared on five charges but found guilty and fined on two counts. He was also banned for life from keeping animals at the shared farm, this ban to apply from a date some two months in the future. This was done because the magistrates, who included a professor of law at the local university, expected Mr Price to appeal. And appeal he did. By then he was no longer conducting his own defence, and it was as well for him that he was now retaining professional advisers.

The appeal judge in the High Court made it clear that he had a very low opinion of Mr Price's activities and would have increased the fine if it had been in his power to do so. As far as the ban was concerned, however, the judge ruled reluctantly that it must be set aside because the magistrates had exceeded their authority when they imposed it. He explained that they could have banned him for life from keeping animals, but by defining a geographical limit to the ban, i.e. the shared farm, they had gone too far.

At that moment in the saga my mind went back to an incident more than a year before. I had been standing in the farmyard with John Price and we were having a bit of an argument. To reinforce a point, I wagged a finger at him and he mistakenly thought I was trying to threaten him physically. He stepped sharply backwards and fell up to his neck in the slurry pit! We pulled him out just as we had pulled out the heifer. It was the only moment of satisfaction I drew from the entire case. Now, with the life ban set aside, we were back to square one. Nothing had been achieved.

The only thing that saved us in the end came about through the slow but persistently grinding progress of natural justice. Put simply, John Price's sins caught up with him. Suppliers to the farm and other people began to foreclose on him; bailiffs arrived and animals were seized and removed from the farm; other animals were sold off to settle various debts, and then quite rapidly the other obstacles tumbled and the whole future of the farm was settled in a generally satisfactory way.

The affair of the shared farm had dragged on over a period of two years, when it could have been settled in weeks. It just shows how deep some family disputes can go, and what misery they can cause others who may be affected by them. In this case the farm animals stood to be the chief losers, and it was surely an appalling situation that for two years no one was prepared to take responsibility for them.

The judge in the High Court said, in his summing-up, that he was fully satisfied that the brother had behaved in the way he did in order to spite his sister. However, he was also satisfied that John Price had been an excellent farmer prior to his change of character, when he had turned from being a humane man into a cruel one. He hoped that the change was temporary.

This was a fair assessment and the judge's final hope was one with which I agreed. However, for the animals whose fate had hung in the balance, the 'temporary' change in Mr Price's character had been perilously long.

The Cat that Would Not

In a village near the sea in West Wales there lived two ladies and their cat. Miss Barrington, Miss Ward and Hector. They were very nice ladies, ever so polite, stalwarts of the church who had retired from England to settle in the Welsh countryside.

I first heard about them because they had a problem which concerned their cat. They had sought the vet's advice, and he had explained that Hector was in pain because he could not urinate when he wanted to. There was a blockage in his bladder, and until this was somehow cleared the vet had to go to the house each day and gently squeeze the cat's bladder to release the urine. Once or twice in the first week, when the vet was busy or had to be away, it fell to me to go to the ladies' house and give the cat his treatment, following written instructions which the vet gave me.

I passed the house every day in any case, and soon a routine developed where I was calling in to attend to the cat more often than the vet. I got to know Miss Barrington and Miss Ward very well, and always I was given tea and a slice of cake. You could not leave that house without your tea and cake.

The other thing about this cat was, it had a wobbly whisker. Unlike all its other whiskers, which sprouted sideways in the proper direction, as straight as the bristles in a new hairbrush, this whisker hung wonkily downwards at an angle of about five o'clock. Healthy whiskers do not do this, so I had a closer look. It turned out that Hector's eccentric whisker was most unhappily sited on the end of an infected root, where it was clearly living on borrowed time. I wondered why the vet had not pulled it out already; he could not have failed to see it. Miss Barrington and Miss Ward knew about it, but they did not want to add to Hector's troubles by grabbing at his whiskers.

I thought about doing it myself. One little tug was all it needed, and the cat's appearance would be much improved, so much more balanced. I was very tempted – just one little tug – and several times I threatened the ladies that I *would* do it, but they only laughed politely and then looked unhappy, so I decided

I was probably intruding on a private matter which really ought to be settled, somehow, between Hector, Miss Barrington and Miss Ward.

One day in the second week of my visits I caught myself in a more determined mood. Miss Barrington and Miss Ward were in the kitchen attending to the tea. I was alone with Hector. I looked at the cat with his wonky whisker, and he looked back at me in, I thought, a sad kind of way.

Right, I said to myself, I'm going to do something about that. The whisker was clearly on the verge of coming out by itself anyway, so I simply speeded the course of history by reaching out and quickly removing it with only the faintest of tugs. A second later, to my great astonishment, the cat began to pee – all by himself, the first time he had managed this for more than two weeks.

It was quite extraordinary, but no fluke. Hector was certainly cured, as he proved very adequately during the next few days. Miss Barrington and Miss Ward were of course delighted when I told them the news – and that day I got more than one piece of cake for my bold initiative.

But had I really done anything? All because of a whisker? Surely not. Surely it was just a coincidence?

CRUFTS AND RUFFS

For some years now, and especially since I have been with the RSPCA, I have come to doubt the validity of dog shows. There are certain happy exceptions, which we will come to later, but the shows that concern me most are, curiously enough, those at the top end of the canine pyramid. And the most famous of these is Crufts.

I should explain that my reservations are not total. Dog shows all adhere to certain basic standards and these by and large are of benefit to the dogs taking part. To stand any kind of a chance, a dog must be well-groomed in advance, which can only be good for it, but there is more to being a successful show dog than having a nice coat.

In 1987 I paid my first visit to Crufts. It is an enormous and hugely famous show, the premier event for pedigree dogs, known all over the world. While I was there I came across a group of visitors who had come from a town in Germany where they belonged to a local owners' club. They all owned German Shepherds, or Alsatians as we usually call them, and they were tremendously enthusiastic about the show. So were a number of other visitors I spoke to who had come along, either by themselves or with a club to see the beautiful dogs on show. And, let there be no doubt about it, some of the dogs there were brilliant; their condition was quite superb.

That, however, is not the principal issue. The thing that concerns me most is what happens to these dogs when they go home. How commercial are the interests of their owners? Do they not in some instances use their dogs as breeding machines? Do the dogs really receive the warmth that ordinary owners give to their pets, whether they are pedigree dogs or belong to that less auspicious breed, the mongrel?

While I was at Crufts, I made it my business to ask one or two people where their dogs slept when they were at home. To my surprise, or rather, as I had suspected, I found that a lot of the dogs lived outside. They either had a kennel to sleep in or a shed which, although probably more palatial than the quarters of the average backyard dog, were nonetheless outdoors. These dogs did not sleep, or live, in the house like an ordinary pet. I challenged someone about the wisdom of this, and they replied:

'Oh, but they need to live outside. For their coats. Their coats have to be kept thick and in the best condition. If you bring them inside, and bed them down in a centrally heated house with all the mod. cons, their coats never look so healthy.'

This confirmed my suspicion that some of these top pedigree dogs were not being treated as pets ought to be treated. They were, if you like, 'kept' animals. Their purpose in life was dictated by owners who wanted them (a) to perform at shows, and (b) to make money.

There are exceptions to this pattern, of course, with owners who let their dogs live in the house and treat them firstly as pets and only secondly as show dogs from which they breed. But the over-riding impression I got from talking to owners at Crufts was that they kept dogs for business reasons. It was therefore important that their animals appeared regularly at shows *and* did well in them, preferably winning their class or at least putting in a good performance each time they came out.

Another thing I noticed: it was by no means always the owner who paraded the dog in the ring. Nowadays there is an ever-increasing army of professional dog-handlers who do this job for the owner; in return they may take a cut of any prizes won, or make some deal or other with the owner which makes it just that bit more important that the dog does well.

I am not claiming for a moment that all owners are like one woman there I spoke to on this subject. I asked her why she allowed her dog to be handled by someone else. 'Well, it bites me,' she said.

It does make you wonder. All right, it's quite funny, but it does make you think about the kind of relationship that existed between dog and owner. What's more, if the handler was that much more effective, you begin to wonder what methods were being used to bring about this obvious 'improvement'. In the final analysis, it is rather sad that fine pedigree dogs have to be owned and treated in this way, the course of their lives dictated by how well things are going at the bank.

RUFF DIAMONDS

For a glimpse of a completely different world, I went one day to Ruffs, where the competitors were all mongrels. The event was billed as a 'fun day' and that is exactly what it was.

There were no professional carry-ons at Ruffs; no petty jealousies or snobberies, and no dog-handlers. Every owner paraded his or her own pet, from the little boy aged eight to the gallant old man of seventy-four, and each was notable in his or her own way. In the case of the eight-year-old, I was much impressed by the way he let the dog take *him* for a walk in the ring, rather than the other way round. This was a novel approach, but they both did very well: every so often the dog would stop to let the lad catch up with him. I thought they had a fine partnership going for them.

The nice thing about the old feller was how he got to the show at all. He lived about twenty-five minutes along the motorway from Scunthorpe, where the event was being held. He had no transport, but he had promised his pet – a little cross-bred terrier called Scruff – that he was going to get him there. He might have been able to catch a bus on an ordinary day, but the event was scheduled for a Sunday and that was much more difficult. So he wrote to the organizers and they put out a plea for someone to give him a lift. He had eighteen offers from people who were only too happy to take him along, free of charge, and not one of them was concerned in the slightest that his dog might be better than theirs, and beat them.

He got to the hall, and his first action was to take his dog into a quiet corner. He pulled out a flask from his bag, and poured a big helping of warm soup into the dog's bowl and gave it to him to drink. The bond between this ageing dog – he was about nine, or sixty-three in human terms – and his seventy-four-year-old owner was something to see.

They didn't win, but they didn't do too badly either. The dog came third in his class, which was for RSPCA Rescued Dogs. In all there were about 140 rescued dogs at the show out of a total entry of around 200. There were classes for Best Rescued Dog, Best Rescued Bitch, Most Appealing Dog, Most Appealing Bitch, Best Condition Dog and Best Condition Bitch. All the winners went forward to a final and the Supreme Ruff turned out to be a nice little cross-bred Collie.

It was a thoroughly marvellous day. Everyone seemed to be in a particularly good mood; the camaraderie was strong from start to finish, with no one-upmanship at all. Here at Ruffs people helped each other out, lending bits of equipment and all waiting their turn without a murmur. And any little accidents of Nature were instantly dealt with by a Keep Britain Tidy team who rushed up with their little shovels, mops and disinfectant.

By comparison with the pedigree shows, I felt that Ruffs had all the good, sensible qualities that we should encourage in dog ownership, and avoided all the excesses that you meet when a couple of doggie eyelashes out of place may cost the owner several thousand quid.

At Ruffs the owners do the grooming at home, before they set out for the show. Pets may receive a bit of a brush before they go in the parade ring but there is none of that frantic scrubbing, powdering and teasy-weasying to make its fur fluff out or its teeth sparkle that you get in the fancy shows. Nor, at Ruffs, do the dogs have to stand in those awful, regimented breed positions which look so unnatural. You know the kind of thing I mean: tail bolt upright in the air, nose Hoovering the floor, ears sticking out at right-angles and all that business.

To me, Ruffs has got the recipe right. It is giving Real Dogs a share of the bright lights at last – and the dogs themselves are lapping it up!

BIG OLIVE

I knew it was going to be one of those days when, just after nine o'clock, I took a telephone call at the Animal Home from a flustered lady.

'Can you come quick?' she said. 'A squirrel has just run up my back passage.'

I conquered a strong urge to giggle and replied: 'Yes, madam. Now where exactly did this happen?'

In vain. The line went dead; we were cut off. With no name, address or even a telephone number I had no alternative but to leave the lady and the squirrel to their respective fates.

I was reporting the essence of this conversation to the others in the office, and they had just begun to offer one or two interesting speculations on the subject, when a booming voice from the reception area silenced us all.

'I've come for the Bloody Dog,' it bellowed.

No one present in the office needed to be told that this voice belonged to the dreaded Big Olive. A sudden transformation overtook the staff of the Animal Home. Just a few seconds ago they had been eager to discuss the problems of the lady with the squirrel. Now they were so busy that none could be spared to go into Reception and deal with Big Olive. Some found that they were urgently needed down at the kennels or in the kitchens. The ambulance driver remembered that he had an injured animal to pick up – or was it a bundle of old newspapers for use in the kennels? Whichever it was, he must be off. The room emptied until only the manageress and I were left.

I had no reason to feel involved. I was just visiting the Animal Home and it was not my job to deal with visitors. The manageress, however, seemed in no hurry to attend to this particular caller. In fact, we had already begun to eye each other with a certain suspicion when the voice we all feared gave tongue once more.

'Anybody in? I want my Bloody Dog!'

A moment later the telephone rang. The manageress and I, now wide-eyed with alarm, rushed to take the call. There were no holds barred in this race to lay hands on the telephone receiver, and I lost. The manageress, clinging tightly to her prize with one hand, placed the other across the mouthpiece and smiled at me; a glint of triumph shone in her eyes, and in a voice calculated to make me feel she was so rushed off her feet she would really appreciate my co-operation, said:

'Chief, would you be so kind as to see whoever that is at the desk for me.'

That's good, I thought: 'Whoever that is at the desk.' She knew only too well who it was. I nodded, not very gracefully, and braced myself for an encounter with the awesome Olive.

I had dealt with Olive before; at some time or other we had all had that privilege. Olive regularly attended the local hospital, going there for spells of treatment which usually lasted several days. Sometimes she went in as a voluntary patient, and at other times the authorities took her in for their own reasons. On this occasion she had been taken in after throwing several stones and a hammer through a neighbour's window. When it became necessary for Olive to go into hospital, her dog often went to stay at the Animal Home and that is how we knew her.

I opened the door to Reception, and there she was. Six feet tall and some eighteen stone in weight. It was Olive, all right, but I was quite unprepared for the incredible costume she was wearing that day. She had wrapped herself in a hospital dressing gown which hung open at the front to reveal what appeared to be an operating theatre gown. Travelling downwards, my eyes noted theatre socks and a pair of worn-out slippers held onto her feet by strips of bandage. On her head she wore a battery of curlers, and these were encased in a ragged piece of star-spangled fabric that once may have passed as a headscarf. A lighted cigarette hung down at one side of her mouth.

It was against the rules of the Animal Home for people to smoke in the reception area, but I had no strong desire to tempt fate by telling Big Olive to 'put it out'. For the time being, too, I kept the reception counter between myself and her. Sometimes she could be quite easy to deal with, but at other times, well, sparks could fly.

Big Olive glared at me. 'You've taken your bloody time,' she said, adding, 'I've come for the Dog. I want to see him.'

Big Olive loved her dog, a cross-bred brindled animal, overweight and temperamental like his owner. Apart from his weight and volatile tendencies, the dog was usually in good condition and well cared for. The problem with Olive was that sometimes she forgot to feed him and at other times she would feed him continually, forgetting that she had already done so.

There was no doubt that the dog returned Olive's devotion. In fact, they deserved each other, and had much in common. If 'The Dog', as Big Olive called him, had started going about with a cigarette drooping from the corner of his mouth, I would not have been surprised.

I sensed that she was in one of her more agreeable moods, so I ventured out from behind the counter. No attack came, and I was able to persuade her to sit down while I explained that the staff were all very busy but just as soon as someone was free they would take her down to the kennels to see 'The Dog'. I fetched her a cup of tea and then went back to the office where the manageress was busy with some paperwork, or so she said.

I telephoned the hospital and told the staff nurse about her missing charge. She was most relieved and promised to send an ambulance down to the Animal Home immediately.

Big Olive was still calmly waiting in a corner of the room for someone to take her to the kennels when another familiar face arrived in Reception. It was that of Mrs Willoughby, a very well-spoken lady of advanced years who saved up her 1p pieces for the RSPCA. She put them in a collecting box and when the box was fairly heavy she would (as the state of the label always betrayed) carefully open the box and, presumably, count the money. Then she would re-seal the label and take the box down to the Animal Home where she would hand it in, saying: 'I don't know how much is in here, dear. Would you count it for me, put a new label on and give me a receipt, please.'

This was one of Mrs Willoughby's handing-in days. She gave the box to the manageress (who by now had surprisingly finished all her urgent work) and was waiting to receive it back with a new label and a receipt when the outer doors of the reception area flew open and in rushed two ambulancemen, followed by two male attendants wearing hospital whites. Without so much as a 'by-your-leave', the two men in the whites each took hold of an arm belonging to frail old Mrs Willoughby and carried her, politely protesting, out of the building and up the steps to where the ambulance was waiting.

'Young man, where are you taking me?' Mrs Willoughby

asked one of the men, but he had no time for conversation. His only concern was to propel this little old lady into the ambulance and get her back to the hospital. It did not matter to him that she was beginning to be highly perturbed.

'Young man, would you mind putting me down,' demanded Mrs Willoughby, sensing that her legs were no longer in contact with the ground and also that she was being carried bodily to an unknown destination, very much against her will.

As Mrs Willoughby vanished through the door, Big Olive rose mightily from her seat in the corner. 'What's the matter with her?' she boomed. 'Is she bloody daft or summat?'

I reacted instinctively. 'You sit down, Olive, and shut up,' I shouted, surprising myself. I obviously surprised Big Olive, too, because she did exactly as I had told her.

Now I ran outside and chased up the steps after the two attendants who were just about to load the still-protesting Mrs Willoughby into the ambulance. 'Hey,' I said, catching one of them by the arm, 'you've got the wrong lady.' I hurriedly explained the situation to them. By this time a small crowd had gathered outside the pub opposite to see what all the commotion was about.

Frail old Mrs Willoughby was duly escorted back down the steps into the Animal Home by two apologetic men in whites. Watching them go, the two ambulancemen started roaring and spluttering with laughter, then they followed on behind, eager to see what happened next. Mrs Willoughby was led through the reception area and into the office where she was lowered into a chair and treated for shock.

I arranged for coffee to be brought and handed the steaming cup to Mrs Willoughby. She drank slowly while the two attendants tried to find new ways of apologizing and the ambulancemen did their best to keep their laughter under control.

After a while Mrs Willoughby seemed to be almost back to normal and I even began to wonder if she was not quite enjoying all the attention she was receiving. Eventually I said to the attendants: 'I don't want to hurry you, but don't you think it's time you collected the person you actually came for?'

One behind the other we trooped out to the reception area. Big Olive was nowhere to be seen. Quickly we organized ourselves into search parties and ran off to look for her in the kennels, the cattery, the offices upstairs, the yard and the toilets. Everywhere we drew a blank. She had vanished. We went round questioning all the staff but no-one had seen her. It seemed as though, while we were all crowding round Mrs Willoughby in the office, Big Olive had grown bored with waiting and had upped herself and gone on her way.

This latest development appealed enormously to our two merry ambulancemen who burst out laughing again. I looked at them and I remember thinking: 'I'm sure those two would be good in an emergency. At least they would cheer people up.'

The men in white coats were not such happy souls. They had molested an innocent member of the public and had also failed to find the person they were meant to collect and take back to the hospital. I walked up the steps with them, and promised to ring them up if and when Big Olive reappeared at the Animal Home.

One of the ambulancemen actually had tears running down his cheeks as he walked round to the back of the ambulance to close the doors. As he took hold of one of the doors a voice from the interior of the vehicle boomed out:

'About bloody time too! If you don't get a move on, I'll miss mid-morning coffee.'

Unseen by us all, Big Olive had installed herself in the ambulance without waiting to be asked. Not only that, she had laid herself out on a stretcher and covered herself up with a blanket. She had clearly forgotten her reason for visiting the Animal Home; any thoughts she may have had of being briefly reunited with 'The Dog' had been overtaken by later events.

Everyone present burst out laughing as the ambulancemen completed their work, the two attendants climbed aboard, shaking their heads, and the vehicle rolled away.

I never did hear whether Big Olive got her mid-morning coffee. I hope she did; somehow she seemed to deserve it. As for the lady with the squirrel, she did not trouble us again, so I hope that problem was amicably resolved between the two of them.

Teatime with Tortoises

In summer, especially, the life of an RSPCA inspector is rarely his own. When he is not working, he is quite likely to be out judging at a pet show – not one of the big events but a little village show where a local community elects its Best Pet. From my experience of these shows, they should give prizes to some of the owners as well!

About a year ago I found myself standing in at short notice for a colleague. The event was in a forest park near Leeds, and was run by a local community organization. When I got there I found a long queue of adults and children, still waiting to enter their pets. It was obviously going to be a bigger event than I had anticipated.

In the end there were so many entrants, it was decided to divide them into three classes: Best Pet Dog, Best Pet Cat, and Best General Pet. After some delay, which nobody seemed to mind because it was a lovely sunny afternoon, we got started.

The standard was very high, and I was extremely pleased to see how much attention had been given to the grooming and care of the cats and dogs. Although many fine cats had come to the Show, I had no difficulty in picking out the winner of that class. It was a delightful animal called Posh Paws which had been brought along by a young lady aged fourteen from Yeadon.

The dog section was even larger than the one for cats, but here too I was able to pick a clear winner. It was a beautiful black dog called Mindy, and its coat shone brilliantly in the sun. Mindy belonged to a young lad from Bradford.

Now we came to the difficult part: the general section. Entered in this class were hamsters, rabbits, guinea pigs, a ferret called Albert and a lobster called Freddy.

All these pets were clearly much loved and cared for by their young owners, but that did not make my problem any easier. How on earth was I to pick a winner out of that lot? How can a hamster be better, or worse, than a guinea pig or a ferret? As for Freddy the lobster, well!

The cogs in my brain span this way and that as I sought a

solution that would be received as both fair and honest. There was no getting round that lobster, however. I felt I had to do something for Freddy, even if it was only to reward the audacity of the owner for bringing it along. In any case, I had no idea how to judge a lobster. I had never seen a pet lobster before, come to that. It certainly made a change from seeing them in a tank at a restaurant, waiting to be picked out and eaten. Finally, I awarded Freddy a special prize, and chose one of the guinea pigs as Best General Pet. The guinea pig thus qualified to go forward for the grand prize of Best in Show.

I was left then with the task of deciding which animal – the cat, the dog or the guinea pig – was to be the Best in Show. They lined up before me and, after further scrutiny, I decided that for condition, behaviour, and the obvious devotion of pet and owner towards each other I must give the title to Mindy the dog.

All the prize-winners received a rosette and certificate, and I made a special rosette available to the lobster. As to where to pin it, I could not decide – but I kept my fingers well away from Freddy's pincers!

A Very Dressy Occasion

They held a Pet Show at a police headquarters one year, and they asked me down there to officiate. They had one or two intriguing classes at this show – though whether these told us anything about the mental processes of police folk I have been unable to decide.

One class was for Pets Who Looked Most Like Their Owners. This was won by an Afghan Hound, whose lady owner really did look remarkably like him. Can you imagine? Try to picture a cascade of golden hair, a slender body, long furry legs and a pointed nose, and you won't be far wrong!

You may not be surprised to learn that they had a Fancy Dress class as well. A certain lady had entered her dog and bitch dressed up as bride and groom. I was told that the happy couple were husband and wife in every sense, and that puppies could be expected some time within the next sixty-three days.

A young lad turned up in a very convincing costume. He was dressed as a sheikh and in one hand he held a rabbit. I asked him what he had come as, and he replied:

'I'm the Sheikh of Arabbit.'

I gave him a prize for that. Then I found out he was the Chief Inspector's son, so while I had probably done the right thing from my own point of view I am not sure how popular this decision was amongst the other entrants.

TEATIME WITH TORTOISES

I was invited to a house not far from where I live. I smartened myself up and went round there, and the lady of the house opened the door and welcomed me inside. In her living-room that afternoon I took tea with a seventy year-old, a sixteen year-old and a thirteen year-old. They were all tortoises.

I sat on the settee and they were on the floor, but I ate as they ate. We had tomato, lettuce, cucumber, apple, carrot and vitamin supplement. I also had a cup of tea, and I think that was the only thing that made me different from them.

The names of the tortoises were George IV, Lester Piggott and Raymond. When I arrived at the house George IV, the eldest, was reclining in a dignified position that suited his years, while the other two were playing a mountaineering game across the furniture in the living-room. Although this was our first meeting, I had heard a lot about these tortoises. I was especially interested to see how alert they were, particularly the younger ones, at a time when most pet tortoises were preparing for hibernation. George IV, Lester Piggott and Raymond were not like most tortoises, however. They never hibernated.

In the warmer months their quarters were a wire enclosure which extended from the back of their owners' garage into the garden. As winter approached, they were moved indoors into the living-room. On the day of my visit, once tea was served and George IV had shaken off his slumbers, all three tortoises were in fine high spirits and not at all lethargic.

I was also amazed to see that they were better house-trained than many dogs and cats. After they had eaten their tea with hearty enjoyment, each tortoise performed its toilet functions on paper which was laid down for that purpose and then was quickly picked up and disposed of.

It has to be said, if this was not already apparent, that the owners of the tortoises were somewhat eccentric. With this in mind, I was glad that a fourth sheet of paper was not produced for me to perform on. I am not sure how I would have coped with that!

WALKING THE GOAT

'You want to drive along there,' they said. 'You'll see it yourself. Every evening he puts this goat on a lead and takes it out for a walk.'

'You're kidding me,' I said. 'That's one of your shaggy goat stories.'

'No, it's not,' they said. 'Belbroughton Road. You go and see for yourself.'

I didn't quite believe them, but one evening I went all the same. I drove into Belbroughton Road, then pulled into the side and parked.

Several people came by as I sat there, all exercising their dogs. I was thinking how nice it was to see so many responsible dog owners, because each and every animal was kept on a lead. Then another pair approached, and I saw that my informants had been correct: this was no ordinary human-plus-dog combination, this was a boy and a goat!

The goat was in beautiful condition and obviously well cared for. I felt I had to stop the lad and ask him about his unusual pet. He was a polite boy, aged eleven and called Martin, and he was perfectly happy to talk to me. I learnt that the goat was called Mary and was named after the church outside which we were standing. His father was the vicar and he lived in the Church House with his parents, two sisters and a brother. He also told me that they had lots of other animals at home. Shortly afterwards, we parted company and I drove back to my house.

That night, I somehow kept thinking about all the animals in the vicarage. I could not get them out of my mind, and so next morning, filled with curiosity, I went round there again. I met the vicar's wife, together with Martin and his brother and sisters, and they showed me the animals that had become part of the household at St Mary's Church.

In the garden was a large run which had been constructed with the help of the churchwarden. It had housing for the various pets and contained ten chickens, two ducks, a tortoise and four rabbits. There was also, in addition to the goat, an Airedale terrier and two cats. At one time or another these animals had all been taken in and added to the household. The ducks (Mavis and Ada) came to them when Martin was out one day with Mary the goat and a lady had approached them. Behind her waddled two ducks and she asked Martin if he would take them over as she could no longer look after them. Martin discussed it with his parents, and the ducks were in.

What was so good about this family was that they obviously took a lot of trouble to learn as much as they could about all the different types of animal they kept, so that none of them should want for anything. I have rarely seen such a mixed yet happy bunch of household pets.

The hens, I was sure, repaid the kindness shown to them with eggs, and perhaps the ducks would one day do the same. The hens, by the way, were named after various ladies in the church congregation. I tried to imagine the scene one Sunday morning, with all those good ladies singing *All Things Bright and Beautiful* at the tops of their voices while, just a few feet away, their namesakes pecked contentedly for corn on the floor of their run.

OUR DAY OUT

As so often happens, when I think of a particular animal I am also reminded of one like it. So, on this occasion, one goat leads to another.

I went along one night to a performance of a play called *Our Day Out*. It was at the Leeds Playhouse, and I have seldom enjoyed an evening at the theatre so much.

I was interested in the play for two main reasons. Firstly, it had animals in it, and secondly some of the performers were pupils from a school near my home and I wanted to see how good a performance they gave.

Now, in general, I am against the use of animals for public performances. Not just because of what happens in the ring or on the stage – it is more complicated than that. So, on the morning before the opening night I called at the theatre in my official capacity to check on the accommodation that had been arranged for the animals.

I need not have worried. The caring staff at the Playhouse had thought of everything, even to the extent of fixing up a perch for two bantams to roost on. There were hutches raised off the floor for the rabbits, and the guinea pigs were equally well housed with plenty of warm dry bedding. The goat looked in excellent condition and arrangements had been made for her to receive plenty of exercise. Two of the rabbits belonged to a member of the theatre staff, and the other animals all came from a local urban farm to which they were to return each weekend during the play's run. The theatre had also made sure that veterinary advice was on hand.

You may be wondering what sort of a play this was that needed such an assortment of animals. Well, it was about a group of children who went on an outing to the zoo, and who in one scene stole all the animals from Pets' Corner.

This was quite a short scene, and sensitively handled. I suppose they could have used toy or stuffed animals for the scene, but afterwards I agreed that it would have spoilt the effect to have, say, a toy goat pulled across the stage on wheels. Besides that, I really did have the feeling that the animals – and especially the goat – were enjoying the fuss being made of them. Rabbits and guinea pigs love to be handled and stroked in any case, and the goat clearly appreciated that she was being given an opportunity to star such as she would never receive down on the farm.

The children in the play all looked after their charges with great kindness and enthusiasm. What they achieved at the theatre was very far from the exploitation of animals that you find in other places. The play, *Our Day Out*, was a genuine learning experience from which I was sure that all would benefit.

Kindness Never Takes a Holiday

Magaluf, as many of you will know, is a holiday resort not far from Palma in Majorca. Like many holiday resorts in that part of the world, the town has a large cat population whose members seem to rely for their survival on handouts of food from British visitors.

The coats of these optimists are usually coarse and flea-ridden. The cats are very thin and unkempt, but mentally they are very alert. They are masters of punctuality, appearing at just the right moment to receive gifts of food which has been smuggled out of hotel dining rooms by their temporary benefactors, over from Great Britain for a week or a fortnight.

I went there for a holiday with my wife, and we noticed that one particular little girl at our hotel was taking considerable amounts of food out of the dining room and giving it to the local cats. She was a pretty girl and she had developed an unusually close relationship with the cats. They showed no fear of her and allowed her to fondle them and feed them by hand. For her age she certainly knew how to handle them.

It then came as a very pleasant surprise to learn that we British do not hold a monopoly when it comes to kindness to animals. This five-year-old girl was from Norway, and she spent almost her entire holiday caring for the cats. I decided I would try and get to know her better, so I asked her guardian about her. At first we had a problem because I did not speak Norwegian and she did not speak English. However, we both knew enough German for me to be able to find out what I wanted to know.

The girl was called Cicilie Furulund, and I also wrote down her address and promised to send her a copy of an article I was going to write about her for the Junior Post section of the *Yorkshire Evening Post*. Meanwhile, my wife Sue and I joined Cicilie in feeding the cats. As we got to know them better, we gave them names which we made up between us. There was Stumpy Eddy, for example, so named because of his tail, who defended his territory against another male called Harry.

We noticed that a female cat, the mother of some young

kittens, had a growth which seemed to be bothering her. This caused us some concern; we felt we should try and get something done about her. In Majorca the RSPCA has an affiliation with an organization called the Centro Canino International. This is run by British ladies who keep a sanctuary for stray and injured animals.

Among their supporters are the Mays, a British family consisting of Jenny and Terry and their teenage daughters Mandy and Sammy. They run Cockney Harry's store in Magaluf. To help the cause of the animals they organize raffles and persuade British visitors to leave behind books which they can sell and give the proceeds to the animal sanctuary. This caring family has rescued some twenty animals, including a dog that suffered a broken back after it was thrown from a balcony.

We turned to the Mays to see if they could help with this black mother cat which had the growth. They agreed to contact the animal sanctuary who would arrange for the cat to be collected and treated.

It was heartening to think that there were such caring people living in a town where the locals took very little care of their animals – and even thought it was daft if someone showed a little kindness towards a cat, or a dog, or a poor old overladen donkey. All I can say is, I am glad there is a regular supply of daft people going out there each year to take care of – and save – the kittens and cats.

— PEOPLE WITHOUT PETS —

I feel sorry for people who can't keep pets, whether for medical reasons or because their landlord won't allow it; sometimes people refuse to have a pet because they think they are too old to cope with a new animal. It is sad when this happens, but there are many ways of getting round the problem.

Here in Leeds we are lucky to have a group of forward-looking Council officers who are responsible for providing leisure facilities for the public. Their imaginative approach has already given us, for example, an urban farm to which children from the city can go and observe the ways of cows, pigs, ducks, and other farm animals; they can spend whole days there, and if they go often enough they can virtually adopt one particular animal as their own. If you are near Leeds, it's called the Meanwood Urban Valley Farm. There are others like it around the country and it's the kind of development that I hope other Councils will feel encouraged to go in for. City children can all too easily be confined within their own little network of streets and buildings; the years go by and suddenly they are fifteen or sixteen and they've hardly ever seen a cow!

On the edge of the city we have Temple Newsam Park, where they keep rare breeds of various animals. It is very pleasant to go there and see unusual types of British cattle, or pigs like the Gloucester Odd Spot, or the goats. Visitors can watch the goats being milked, and see yoghurt being made from the milk. Again, like the urban farm, this park is offering a valuable contact with the countryside to people whose normal vistas are dominated by brick and concrete blocks.

JUMPING TERRAPINS!

Readers who have seen the *Animal Squad* series may recall the episode where I and a posse of my colleagues spent many fruitless minutes trying to guess which way a terrapin would jump off a piece of floating wood so we could capture it in our net. We were beside this pool for more than an hour altogether, and eventually we had to go away empty-handed.

The terrapin was too clever for us. After much discussion we decided, from the way it was facing, that it would jump to the left. Very gently and gingerly we lowered the net on the end of a long pole, and set it in position. At the very moment the net touched the water the terrapin made its move, leaping backwards into the pool and disappearing into some reeds. End of rescue mission.

We had been called out originally because someone had reported seeing a terrapin living in a pool near a power station. It had obviously been dumped – the fate of many terrapins – and although it had adapted surprisingly well we were concerned that it would not be able to cope for much longer with the very cold water temperature in the pool. Now, thanks to another Council project, we had very much better accommodation to offer the city's abandoned terrapins, and that is where our elusive friend would have gone had he chosen to jump into our net.

This new refuge is the terrapin pool at Roundhay Park. It is part of an ambitious aquarium scheme which is being built with the help of the Community Programme; when completed, it will be far ahead of its time. Already there are large ponds where dozens of beautifully coloured carp swim about in their leisurely way. Visitors can wander round the ponds along a series of wooden walkways in a lush, warm conservatory atmosphere. Bananas and oranges grow on nearby trees.

In the tanks near the present entrance you can come face to face with many wonderful aquatic animals, including a crocodile and a Nurse Shark. Not a lot of people get very close to sharks in their lifetime, but you can at Roundhay Park. This shark is outgrowing his present accommodation but soon he will be moved to a spacious new tank where the water will be changed every hour to provide superb conditions.

Anything that recalls a zoo or circus atmosphere is carefully avoided. There are no performing animals; the ponds and tanks are more like homes to their inhabitants, many of which were 'donated' by local people who, for one reason or another, were unable to keep them. I use the word 'donated' in quotes because some of the animals were dumped, but now at least they have good homes and can give pleasure to thousands of people who otherwise might not have had the chance to admire and get to know them. With facilities like these, and the others at the urban farm and the rare breeds park, no one need miss the experience of having a pet because they can always go and see some animal that appeals to them.

People often do not realize at the outset how difficult it is to keep aquatic animals. The terrapin pool has a resident population of around fifty, nearly all of which were abandoned or handed in by local people, and until a larger space becomes available the park manager has recently had to draw the line and refuse to take any more.

The trouble begins at the pet shops. It is so easy to buy a nice little terrapin and take it home. 'Where will it live?' someone asks. 'Oh, I hadn't really thought about that. Still, shouldn't be difficult. They live in water, don't they? We'll get it a tank.'

In fact, terrapins like to spend a lot of time *out of the water*, basking on a rock in a warm, light atmosphere. They also need feeding regularly, and, like almost any animal you can think of, they grow bigger. Soon the typical terrapin is too large for the tropical fish tank in which it has been placed. Then the owner hears a rumour that terrapins can give you salmonella poisoning. He doesn't like that one bit; in fact he gets in a bit of a panic. A couple of nights later, he fills a plastic carrier bag with water, slinks out with the terrapin and drops it in the river. 'Goodbye, Terry. Best of luck, mate,' he tells it. If Terry *is* lucky, he ends up at somewhere like Roundhay Park.

This brings me to the sad topic of goldfish. It horrifies me each time I see a child coming back from the fair with a goldfish in a plastic bag. All too well I know what will happen next. The goldfish spends the next day or so swimming around in a sink, or is dropped into a jam jar. Then, once someone has been to the shop, the new arrival is given its very own goldfish bowl. This is placed on the window-sill, without any weeds or other vegetation in it. The goldfish is completely exposed to the light; having no eyelids, it has no way of getting any rest, and its daily existence becomes a slow torture. No wonder so many goldfish have short lives.

If people must keep goldfish at home, then the least they should do is provide a large tank with proper filtering equipment. The tank should be sited in a part of the room which receives only a limited amount of direct sunlight and should be furnished with a gravel base with weeds and a piece of rock so the goldfish always has somewhere shady to go. Better still, though, let the goldfish live outdoors in a lake or pond where it has plenty of space to swim around.

At Roundhay Park the Council have installed a marvellous pool for their goldfish. Other Councils are pursuing the same route and I can only applaud them. The fish do so well in these surroundings, which are designed to be as close to the goldfish's natural environment as it is possible to make them. They grow so big, and stay so fit, that there must be something about this method which is so much better than confining them to a little bowl in someone's house, where the owner may get tired of them and their life loses much of its purpose.

So, finally, to anyone who is thinking of acquiring a goldfish, I would say this: if you have any doubts about your ability to install the very best equipment, or about the amount of time you are prepared to give to feeding and caring for the fish, then, please . . . try your local park instead.

— THE DOG THAT DROVE —
—— THROUGH CUSTOMS ——

One spring day in 1976 a French family drove their car off the ferry at Folkestone. The father, Guy Martel we will call him, was driving; with him in the car were his wife, his younger brother and his twelve-year-old daughter. Also in the car, sitting on the back seat in full view, was a dog.

At the passport window, the Martels handed over their documents for inspection. These included an EEC dog passport and a rabies vaccination certificate. The official looked briefly at the documents, stamped them – including the dog passport – and handed them back to their owners. Uniformed men waved the car through and the Martel family, complete with dog, began their holiday in Britain.

Incredible, you say? Just hold on a minute. Three days later, a woman in North Wales saw some French people exercising their dog. She became suspicious and telephoned the Ministry of Agriculture, Food and Fisheries to report that a dog may have been imported illegally into the country in contravention of the anti-rabies laws.

After the Martels had been in Britain for seven days, I received a telephone call from the police asking me to go to the local police station at a town in West Wales. I was told about the French family and their dog, and that the Ministry had been informed but nothing had been done so far. I thought for a moment and replied, remembering something I had heard at a conference, that this was not really an RSPCA matter. I suggested that the police got in touch with the Ministry and asked them to sort it out. Unfortunately the divisional veterinary office had no one available to work on the case and the buck was passed back to me. Seven days had gone by and it was becoming increasingly urgent to establish whether the dog was rabid or not, and so I agreed to contact the family.

The Martels had booked into a small hotel, and when I found them they made no attempt to conceal the dog from me. They appeared genuinely to think that they had obtained all the right documents to bring their family pet with them on holiday to

Britain. In addition to the EEC dog passport and the rabies vaccination certificate, they had a letter from a French vet stating that he had examined the dog and found it to be free from infection and disease. Of course, the dog passport is not valid for Britain, and I was surprised that the Martels did not know that. I was also surprised that they had not noticed or reacted to any of the anti-rabies warning signs that are posted at various points on all cross-Channel ferries. Be that as it may, here they were in West Wales with their dog; what were we going to do with them?

When the authorities did at last come to life, they behaved with an odd mixture of bureaucratic high-handedness and casual indifference. The Martels, whether they deserved it or not, were in for a hard time over the next few days.

The first step was to examine the dog and I called in a vet to do this. He was satisfied that the dog was free from infection but he also said that it would have to be kept in isolation until the Ministry took action. He then went off to report his findings to the Ministry who were still showing little interest even though their offices were less than a mile away.

The next thing I heard was via the police. Someone from the Ministry had telephoned the police station, giving an order that the dog should be placed in *my* vehicle, and that the vehicle should be locked and left outside the police station. This I refused to allow for several reasons. If the dog developed an infection, it would be better to leave it where it was. I certainly did not want my van to be placed in isolation for an indefinite period. The best solution was to have a secure cage sent over from Carmarthen in which the dog could be kept while it was transported to wherever the authorities decided it should eventually go.

The Ministry's response was to agree to this but to insist that the dog should be moved from where it was and placed in isolation outside the police station until the secure cage arrived. I suggested that the best vehicle to use was Monsieur Martel's own car, and after a lot of argument and discussion this was agreed and done. During the afternoon I fed the dog while we waited for the cage to arrive; it finally came after six hours had passed – not very rapid going for a half-hour journey. The dog was installed in the cage and taken off to Carmarthen.

That evening a special court was convened in the town. Monsieur Martel appeared before the magistrates and was fined £500. No time was set to pay and the defendant's passport was returned to him and he was given the name of an official carrier who would transport the dog back to Folkestone for a further charge of £80. After the hearing the French family had nowhere to go so I took them back to my house and gave them some tea. My French is not up to much and I asked the local university to find me an interpreter so we could try to unravel the problems facing the Martels.

They were originally given three options over the dog's future. Either they could have it shot; or they could have it put in quarantine for six months, or they could return with it direct to France. They chose this last option, but it proved impossible to organize this for them. I tried to enlist the help of the French consular office in Carmarthen but they, beyond offering their sympathy, did not want to know. Then the Ministry changed their mind and said the dog could not go back to France immediately; it would have to remain in Britain for at least fourteen days. I could not see the logic behind this, and it certainly did not appear consistent with the six-month quarantine regulations. That, however, was the Ministry's decision and they were sticking to it.

By now Monsieur Martel was growing distinctly alarmed for the safety of his dog; he was even beginning to doubt that it was still alive. I tried to reassure him as best I could but the idea had taken shape in his head that the crafty British had gone behind his back and destroyed his dog. To add to the family's problems, they had very little money left and would not be able to wait in Britain for the full two weeks. I suggested that they might do better to return home, get the necessary funds together for the release of the dog and then come back and collect it.

Monsieur Martel then asked if he could see his dog. This I arranged, and next morning I gave him a Ministry note authorizing the people in Carmarthen to produce the dog when he arrived there. Off he went. The next thing I heard was that he had been arrested in Carmarthen on a charge of attempting to leave the country without paying a fine!

This upsetting and quite unnecessary turn of events had come about because when the fine was imposed the magistrates' clerk, who was new to the job, had failed to realize that Britain had no reciprocal arrangement with France for getting a fine paid if the person left the country. Monsieur Martel was therefore detained until another court could be convened to look into his means and establish how the fine must be paid. This court agreed to accept £50 within seven days and the responsibility for making that payment was left with the defending solicitor.

The Martels' story was now becoming known to a wider audience, and although the father could barely raise £25 by himself a collection was taken amongst well-wishers and this made up the balance owing. People contributing to this fund did not want to condone the offence of bringing the dog into the country, but they seemed to recognize that a lot of unfortunate things had happened to the family – and to the dog which, after all, was little more than an innocent bystander in an international mix-up.

Monsieur Martel and his family returned to France. He kept his word and on the appropriate day came back to England to settle his debts and collect his dog. They finally set sail for France – and I shall be very surprised if I ever see them again.

Several important issues were raised by this affair. Firstly, there should be much tighter controls at Britain's ports. It was a truly extraordinary lapse for one of our Immigration officials actually to stamp the dog's EEC passport without realizing what he was doing. That, however, is no guarantee that it will not happen again.

If and when a Channel tunnel is built, the risk of animals coming here undetected will be very much greater and we must be prepared to make a lot more effort to keep Britain a rabies-free country. The risk extends also to wild animals, and I am thinking particularly of rats which will be very hard to shut out as they make their way along the tubes and tunnels from France. We have enough trouble through rats escaping from ships in our docks, and the problem will be infinitely greater and harder to control once a land link with Europe is in existence.

What also emerged from the affair was that, should something like it happen again, we need to have a more positive and more efficient approach worked out to deal with it. As it was, our officials were unnecessarily high-handed and the family were caused a lot of distress. They spoke almost no English and, although they had the services of an interpreter, the events in

— RABIES —
SOME FACTS ABOUT THIS FATAL DISEASE

Rabies is caused by a virus which attacks the central nervous system.

The virus is often present in the salivary glands, and may be spread by an infected animal biting another, the virus passing into the fresh wound.

If the virus comes into contact with torn nerve fibres, it travels up them to the spinal cord, and is transmitted to the brain.

All warm-blooded animals can be infected. Although rabies is widely thought of as the 'Disease of the Dog', all animals which naturally use their teeth for offence and defence are at risk.

In some countries, wild animals infect humans in significant numbers. The wolf, hyena, jackal, wild cat, mongoose and fox are just some of the animals known to spread rabies in this way.

Rabies is not present in Britain, but all animal bites suffered in other countries must receive immediate medical treatment. Cleansing with soap and water can help to remove some or all of the virus, and serum or vaccine treatment can be effective if given within twenty-four hours of infection. It has little, if any, effect if given three or more days after infection.

court must have been very bewildering to them. They also had to cope with the frightening experience of being split up when the father was arrested, and at several stages I am sure they must have wondered if they would ever see their home in France again.

Some weeks after the Martels had finally returned home, various questions were asked in Parliament about the provisions available should an outbreak of rabies occur in this country. The replies were not very encouraging to those who understand what they really meant, and I think it is fair to say that the Government has not changed its position to this day. Rabies is a low-priority matter and will be kept that way until something happens. I think they have got it wrong.

LIVE ON STAGE

Ozzie Osbourne and his Heavy Metal band were due to play in Leeds, and their reputation for wild behaviour on the stage had gone before them. It was said that Ozzie Osbourne himself had bitten the head off a bat during a concert in the United States. Another of his gimmicks was throwing offal at his audience.

In Leeds the City Council were very wary of the effect that such a performer might have on the local audience, and the band were ordered to leave certain parts out of their act. I was called in to make sure that there was no repetition of the bat incident, or anything like it involving animals.

I went down to the Queen's Hall, a vast concert hall on the site of the old bus depot. I got there early, long before the audience were due in, and had a look round. I must have seemed out of place because a feller came up to me and said: 'I think you might need this.'

'What is it?' I asked.

'Well,' he said, 'you haven't got any ear-plugs but I think you're going to need some cotton wool.'

With that he handed me a wad of the stuff and suggested I make my own sound-proofing arrangements. It turned out that he was in charge of the St John Ambulance unit that would be looking after people who fainted or did themselves an injury from too much head-banging. I told him why I was there – it was no good pretending I was there out of admiration for Ozzie Osbourne, even if I *had* dressed up in casual clothes so I wouldn't attract unwanted attention.

'Oh, aye,' said the feller. He seemed to understand my slight problem with the age and culture gap, because he added: 'If you get fed up when it starts, our caravan's out the back.'

'Thank you,' I said.

If I had any doubts about the need for cotton wool in the ears, these were instantly blown away by the support band when they appeared on stage and started giving the PA system a very vigorous workout.

In the meantime I had gone to have a word with Ozzie Osbourne's manager.

'Look,' I said, 'please, let's have no funny business tonight with any animals.'

He gave me one of those born-again-choirboy looks. 'I'll tell you,' he said, 'I'm glad you've come. I'm really glad.'

What was this? I wondered. Was he going to tell me that he and the boys had turned over a new leaf and wanted to join the RSPCA? Not quite. The reason for his joy on seeing me in the theatre was a trifle more commercial.

'You have been marvellous for us,' he said. 'The best thing we have ever had. All that free publicity . . . it's been great.'

I was aware that the confrontation with the City Council had been a popular story in the newspapers, but I was surprised to hear that the band's chief representative on earth thought they had actually done well out of it! Alas, the art of luring large numbers of bottoms on to theatre seats is not one of my specialities. Anyway, the manager earnestly promised that there would be no 'naughty stuff' that night, and I went out front to enjoy the concert.

At least, I think I enjoyed it. It was certainly different. A couple of the songs were quite nice, really. There was also the bit where someone threw a rubber bat at me from the stage. Just trying to be friendly, I suppose.

Twiggy: The One that Got Away

We have already met Freddy, the fox who was caught in a snare in a back garden on the outskirts of Leeds (see 'Foxes in the City'). As you can imagine, if people are going to set these horrible traps next to their own houses, they will very likely ensnare domestic animals as well. A neighbour's cat or dog may easily be the next victim.

This particular type of snare is not in fact illegal, however unpleasant it may be. It consists of a length of wire, anchored at one end and with a running noose at the other. When the animal steps into the noose and puts pressure on the wire, the noose pulls tight. The more the animal tugs and jerks at the wire, the tighter it gets. Few animals escape by their own efforts alone, although I have heard horrific stories of foxes who in their agony have tried to gnaw off their trapped leg and thus free themselves at dreadful cost.

I came across an unfortunate cat who had walked into a snare and had been held in the grip of the wire noose for several days. During that time and for some while afterwards she endured a life of misery. She was heavily pregnant when she was trapped, and she actually gave birth to her kittens while a prisoner. Even after that she was still able to overcome her pain and mother her kittens. When they were at last found, all had survived the ordeal.

The life of the mother cat was still by no means safe. She was rushed off to a vet and only then could anyone really see how close she was to death. The wire noose had cut so deeply into her body that it was only millimetres away from her spine. Had it bitten through just that fraction more, she would have been finished; either hopelessly paralyzed or killed.

The vet did marvellously well to release her from the noose without further damage. She and the kittens recovered for a while at the Animal Home and then homes were found for them. No one knew, or was admitting, where the cat had come from. Twiggy, as we called her, was not apparently wild when we found her, although in her weakened state it was difficult to tell what kind of a past she had had. We assumed she had once been someone's domestic pet, but when no one came forward to claim her we took a decision. We crossed off one of her nine lives and set about finding her somewhere to spend the remaining eight.

THE RABBIT GAME

If you talked to the average person about rabbits, they would very likely tell you that, apart from those you can see running across waste ground, or in the wild, a rabbit is a pet, an animal that a child keeps in a hutch in the garage or garden shed.

If you asked them about rabbits for the table, very few would say that they ate rabbit regularly. Those that do usually say that their rabbit comes ready-diced in a freezer bag from the local supermarket.

When asked about the various breeds of rabbit, most people we spoke to while investigating the rabbit trade said that they were kept by specialist breeders for exhibiting at rabbit shows up and down the country. True, there are some specialists who breed and care for particular types such as the New Zealand White, the California, the Carolina, the Dutch and the cuddly Lop, but what came to light during my investigations was that a cottage industry has emerged in which rabbits are bred for their meat and fur.

Many breeders I spoke to did not realize that the rabbits they bred for meat were also being exploited by the dealers for their fur which was sold as coney-fur, for making coats. The breeders received no payment for the fur, and were only getting £1–£1.50 per rabbit for its meat. Most of this meat was processed and sent abroad, mainly to Europe, and France in particular.

A rabbit has a life expectancy of about eight or nine years. Most of the does used to produce rabbits for this market live for about two years, during which time they are forced to produce some 130 young. When they reach this target they have served their purpose, and are discarded. They are considered 'not commercially viable', and they are killed.

The young are taken from the does as soon as possible to be fattened up. This takes about eight weeks and then, according to the instructions issued to the breeders, each young rabbit should weigh about four pounds. When they have reached the correct weight they are sold for meat and fur.

The next stage is for the rabbits to be taken for slaughter. On the way they are subjected to long journeys in vans and the boots of cars until they reach one of the many collection points which are set up round the country. There they are handed over to a carrier who loads them into crates which are transferred to the back of a lorry. They travel in this way for perhaps hundreds of miles to the slaughterhouse.

This form of rabbit trade is not in itself illegal, but many people would object to the callous way it is carried out. I have spent some considerable time watching rabbits being handed over at collection points and then following them to their ultimate destination. The whole of the transport operation leaves much to be desired. The rabbits are handled roughly, for one thing. The carriers lift them by the neck or ears, two at a time, and, without supporting any other part of their body, carry them across and drop them into crates. A lot of the crates I have seen and examined should not have been used; they were broken and had jagged edges which could cause injury to the rabbits inside them or to rabbits in an adjacent crate. When the lorries were loaded, the crates were stacked on top of one another until up to 400 or so rabbits were aboard. In this condition they were driven to the slaughterhouse, badly overcrowded, with urine and excrement finding its way down through the crates from top to bottom.

Many of the rabbit breeders I spoke to said they had lost money on the venture and would be getting out as soon as they could. However, as quickly as one discontented breeder left the trade, another would come into it, lured by the colour brochures and extravagant promises of the companies which set them up in business.

One such newcomer was a seventeen year-old who lived on a smallholding high up in the Yorkshire Pennines. He had not been in work for more than a year and his father worked for the local council as a driver. He was watching a farming programme on television one Sunday which contained a feature on rabbit-breeding. Attracted by the idea, he looked through the newspapers to see which companies were the biggest advertisers. With his father's approval, he sent off for some brochures and soon found himself reading about the very glittering future which awaited anyone who took up breeding rabbits.

'Everyone should remember that a doe can produce £90-worth of income per annum,' said one brochure. It went on to say how easy it was to become a breeder – the perfect answer for people at present unemployed, or who had been made redundant, or were about to retire. Profits were there to be made – and without a lot of work. The brochure emphasized that rabbits grew quickly and needed little attention. No 'sophisticated buildings' were required, in fact 'You do not even need a building at all. Rabbits will thrive outside in the UK with great success if properly housed.'

I take great exception to this line of talk because animals will *not* thrive without good husbandry, and the public are being badly misled by some of these companies. Here is another example of their irresponsible selling techniques.

'We have carefully developed a rabbit which grows rapidly on the minimum amount of feed . . . Rabbit production fits in well on most farms or indeed anywhere a small amount of space is available for the project – even your backyard.'

This again worries me greatly because it encourages a total novice to plunge into the business whether he has suitable premises or not. Someone like that will have very little or no idea how to look out for and deal with the spread of disease. This is particularly important in a food-producing concern, and it seems to me that there is no proper control exercised over these backyard farms. The inspectors from the Ministry of Agriculture, Food and Fisheries do not usually become involved until the slaughterhouse stage, by which time large numbers of the rabbits arriving there could be infected with all kinds of diseases. The way they are packed in crates on the lorries, in mixed consignments, means that disease can spread very quickly from one batch to another.

This was all far from the mind of our young unemployed friend at the beginning of his venture in the rabbit trade. He read the brochures and thought that rabbit breeding would suit him down to the ground. He arranged a loan through the Enterprise Allowance scheme and sent off his order for rabbits and equipment. In his own words, this is what happened next:

'On the 2nd October I went to collect the thirty does and three bucks. Mr X told me we should have a batch of rabbits to go around Christmas and we should leave the rabbits for three weeks to settle down before starting to breed. A month went by and I put one of the bucks with one of the does each night. On the 27th November one doe had five kits and another had six. These eleven babies continued to do well for a week, then on 3rd December when I went to feed the rabbits I found all the babies dead. I contacted our vet and took the babies on to him to be analyzed. His diagnosis was that they died from meningitis.

'It said in the leaflets from [the company] to ring for advice at any time. When I did ring I spoke to Mr X who was very rude and didn't want to know my problem. My Dad then had to ring them as I didn't know what to do. A lady there spoke to him and told him to get a bottle of Duphacillin from our vet and said she shouldn't be telling him about it because it was against company rules but the breeding stock should be injected with it two days before the babies were due.

'After that I tried with ten does to one buck in a large pen. They were very happy and seemed to mate, but after a month nothing had happened. Our vet rang the company's vet who said that they didn't breed from November to January, and he suggested changing the injection to Duplocillin. Our vet visited our premises and examined the rabbits, and said he didn't think any were pregnant. He took away the literature to read up on it and said he would be in touch.

'The company hadn't told us anything about having to inject the rabbits or we would never have bought them. By this time I was very depressed as I had borrowed £1000 to join the Enterprise Allowance scheme and was very worried about how to pay it back. I then rang round different organizations to get advice and the only people that could help me were the RSPCA. They came and filmed the hut in which I keep my rabbits. Our vet called again, then he contacted the company vet once more who tried to put the death of the baby rabbits down to lack of ventilation in the hut, but our vet said there was plenty and that the rabbits seemed very healthy.

'We are left with thirty rabbits which haven't made me a penny in four months of keeping them. I have lost interest and think I have been given a lot of false information. No way would I have bought these rabbits in October and have to wait until March for results. I am very depressed and don't know how I am going to pay back £1000. I have the Enterprise lady coming in March and I still have no litters to show for four months' work. I will have to get something sorted out soon or I won't be able to stay in the scheme.'

On a separate sheet he wrote out how the money had been spent:

'£305 for rabbits
  180 for corn
  329 for cages and breeze-blocks
   60 nestboxes
   30 scales
   35 nails and wood
   20 nipples
    5 company cards
   20 hay
   10 breeding book
   10 telephone
   15 vet kit
   33 paid vet
   30 electric
   50 diesel and petrol
       —————

£1132 – not including labour.'

This lad is by no means alone. Increasingly, as I speak to other backyard breeders, more and more of them feel they have been duped by their suppliers. I have some sympathy for them, of course, but my chief concern is with the suppliers because it is they who dictate the methods and terms of this unpleasant, inhumane trade.

In the meantime, to anyone reading this book who may feel tempted by a newspaper advertisement saying he can expect to earn £90 a year from each doe he keeps, I have just one piece of advice. It's rubbish; please forget it.

STRAY DOGS

In an earlier chapter, 'The Dog That Drove Through Customs', we saw how easily a dog was brought into this country from France, despite all our warnings and anti-rabies laws. In this chapter I want to look at the wider question of how we control our very large dog population, especially the dangerous outlaw element – the strays.

Any dog not under the control of its owner is, strictly speaking, a stray. It may seem hard on some owners to associate the half-wild animals which roam our cities with their nice old Rover – 'He's not a stray, I just let him out for a couple of minutes!' Yes, but in those couple of minutes he could do a lot of damage. He might attack someone, get involved in a fight with another dog, or cause an accident simply by running into the road. Many people don't realize this, and some people don't want to, but the problem of stray dogs is now in need of urgent attention.

To give you an idea of the scale of the problem, it is estimated that for the district of Leeds, which covers the area in and around the city (population 500,000), some 10,000 stray dogs are on the loose at any one time. That figure includes what we call 'latchkey dogs', animals which are put outdoors by their owners when they go out to work, and stay out until the owners come home again. These dogs form packs, and are a very real danger in the community. They are a menace to people living nearby, and they are also a menace to themselves. Should rabies ever take hold in this country, these packs are the main places where the disease could flourish. By then, the only answer will be a massive slaughter of all stray animals.

If we do not tackle this problem soon, we will have huge difficulties in the future. Although rabies is the most frightening of the likely or possible diseases, it is not the only one. Distemper, canine virus hepatitis, leptospiral (kidney) infections – all are killers, and if the dog is not inoculated against them, usually as a puppy, they can easily spread to other dogs it may come into contact with. There are many other weakening infections, such as worms, which can be passed from one dog to another. If we do not urgently take steps to limit the possibilities of infection, we must be prepared for some kind of epidemic to break out.

When this happens, and very large numbers of dogs are taken off the streets and destroyed, there will be a lot of loud and bitter complaints from their owners who will say that any such action is heavy-handed, unnecessary, a crime in itself, etc. The last thing they will ever realize is that they have only themselves to blame.

If all dog-owners were responsible, kept their dogs on leads in public places, fed and cared for them adequately – which includes paying vets' fees when necessary – we should be more than half-way to solving the problem of having a diseased dog population. Going further, we also need a proper system for monitoring dog owners and a full-time dog-warden scheme on a nationwide basis.

The current belief of some politicians is that we do not need dog licences at all. This way of thinking will lead us back to the Dark Ages. We do very much need a licensing system, and the main thing wrong with the present one is not that it costs more to run than the Government can claw back in licence fees. The main thing wrong with it is that we are licensing the wrong animal. We should be licensing the owners, not the dogs.

At present it is too easy for people to disclaim ownership. Say an unlicensed dog has caused an accident; two cars have crashed and a child has been killed. The owner of the dog is traced, but then says: 'No, it's not my dog, it's just one that comes to the house sometimes, and I give it a bit of food.' Ownership cannot be proved in those circumstances, and so there is no onus on that individual to keep his or her dog under control.

Many dog owners I have spoken to would welcome a better licensing system. Instead of paying 37p towards a scheme that costs £1 per dog to run, they are prepared to pay considerably more if that would create a better and safer environment for themselves and their pets. What they want is not unreasonable. They are looking towards the day when they can take their dog out for a walk on its lead without the constant fear that it will be attacked by another dog, or worse, by a pack of strays, and that it will not be so liable to contract a disease from another dog.

If, when the licence was issued, it was made out in the name of the owner, and specified the conditions in which the dog must be kept, this would in my view force the less-than-perfect owner to take a more responsible attitude. He would know that he was accountable, and there would always be the threat in his mind – however distant – that he stood to lose his licence if a dog in his charge went and did something it seriously shouldn't have. Of course, laws already exist to ban people from keeping a dog, but I wonder if we could not devise some more efficient system than one which always involves a court case, possibly lengthy and always expensive.

I would also like to see a much greater extension of the dog-warden schemes which are currently in operation. We have two dog-warden teams in Leeds, and their job is to round up stray dogs. They take them back to the owner and, if this is a first offence, give the owner a warning. Alternatively they can impound the dog and the owner has to go down to the pound and pay a fee to get the dog out; if the dog is not collected in seven days, it can be passed to a new owner, or put down.

What worries me here is that, without a licensing system, a callous owner – and there are some – may refuse to pay the fee, taking the attitude: 'Let them put the dog down. We'll get another one.'

We need to be much tighter in the way we organize and administer our dog-owning laws. I am in favour of having dog wardens, as I mentioned, but they should be on duty all round the clock, not working as they do at present from nine o'clock in the morning until four in the afternoon. The problem of stray dogs is already too big for a part-time solution. Money will have to be spent, but I am convinced that it is in everyone's interests that we should put our hands into our pockets and buy ourselves a better system.

IN THE PUBLIC EYE

I have felt for a long time that it can only help our cause if some of us stand up in public and talk about what we do, or write articles for newspapers, or books like the one you are reading. The publicity we attract helps to create a general awareness of animals and their needs, and this in the long term can only be of benefit to the animal community as a whole.

In the shorter term, the RSPCA is a charity and we naturally appreciate all the donations we receive which help to fund our work. Being a charity is a competitive business these days; with so many worthy organizations in search of income from the public, it must be a good thing if we can keep on popping into your living rooms via the television set to remind you of our existence. Doing it, though, is another matter.

Lately I have made quite a number of appearances on television, in addition to the *Animal Squad* series, and I can only say that show business is another world entirely. Also, you meet some funny people. Let me tell you about the time I went to London to appear on Jimmy Tarbuck's TV show *Live From The Piccadilly*.

I travelled down on the train from Leeds with my wife Sue, and at the station a car was waiting to take us to the theatre. There we were met by a producer who took us inside and introduced us to Little Billy.

'This is Little Billy,' he said, 'he'll look after you while you're in the theatre.'

With that, my bags were whisked out of my hands and off went Little Billy. I did not see him – or the bags – till some while later. In the meantime I wondered who he was, and what he wanted with my bags which contained all my uniform which they wanted me to wear on the show. When I asked someone if I should go and get changed, they said:

'Don't worry. Little Billy will look after everything.'

We went into the hospitality room and I had a drink – a Coke, as I wasn't going to fluff any lines if I could help it. This was a live show and you didn't get a second chance. Then I was taken to meet Jimmy Tarbuck and we discussed our little routine together – it was not a rehearsal as such, we just talked about what we would do. When that was over, Little Billy suddenly appeared.

'Time for you to change, sir,' he said.

I followed him up to my dressing room. We went in, and the first thing I saw was my shirt, laid out on an ironing board. Now, we had pressed that shirt before we left home. I had thought it looked fine, but obviously it wasn't good enough for Little Billy who had pressed it all over again. Each sleeve was immaculately creased. He had even inserted little pegs in the cuffs to keep them together.

I said to him: 'I pressed that before we came out.'

'Never mind, sir,' said Little Billy, as if he was forgiving me for something. 'I'll look after you.'

Then he went on: 'Does sir wear cuff links?'

'No,' I said, 'I don't. Not under a pullover, anyway.'

Little Billy's face was fairly white already. Now it went the colour of a cold semolina pudding. 'What, sir?' he cried. 'What pullover? What pullover? I haven't pressed it, sir. What? Where is it?'

'It's in my other bag,' I said.

'Oh, dear me, sir.' Little Billy seized the bag and opened it and whipped out my uniform pullover. It was on the ironing board before you could say 'Rowenta'. I looked round the room. Where have my trousers gone, I wondered, what's he done with them?

Then I saw them on a coat-hanger, with razor-sharp creases in them. I reckon *I* can press a pair of trousers, but these were amazing.

Then we came to the next phase in the operation. It was time for me to get dressed, or, rather, for Little Billy to dress me!

'Come on, sir, come on,' he was saying, 'take those clothes off.'

He held out the immaculate shirt, opened and ready for me to step into. This had never happened to me before. My very own butler for a day. Right, I thought, in for a penny, in for a pound. I poked my arms backwards – and down the sleeves of the shirt they went. Lovely.

'Thank you,' I called over my shoulder, 'I can do it up myself, thank you.'

Too late, he was round the front, his fingers pecking at the buttons and patting the shirt front to make sure it was beautiful and flat. Next thing, he'd grabbed the coat hanger and was holding out my trousers.

'Step into these now, sir.'

'It's all right, it's all right, I can do it meself.'

'No, sir, no. This way, please.'

'Oh, all right.'

I did as I was bidden. You know, I thought to myself, you could get to like this sort of thing if it happened often enough. I was being waited on like a lord; hand, foot and shirt-front. The works. And that was before we got to the shoes.

The shoes were a revelation by themselves. I had already cleaned them, of course. I had bulled the toes, as I always do; something I have carried over from my army days. But Little Billy had gone to town with them. They were *sparkling*. I could not believe what he had done with them. I looked at myself in the mirror, at the whole ensemble. It was marvellous. I felt like a million, no, a *billion* dollars.

I went downstairs and took my place in the wings, ready to go on. In my hands I held my peaked hat which I had picked up on my way out of the dressing room. All of a sudden a small figure was stood beside me, hissing.

'Sir, you didn't tell me you had a hat, sir,' hissed Little Billy. He snatched it off me, produced a brush from nowhere and a quarter of a second later he was spinning the hat to make the nap all go the same way. When he handed it back, it was better than new. By the time I finally walked on stage I had lost all my fears – of the audience, of what they might think of me, or whether I might make a mistake. I was looking SMART, and I knew it, and everything would be all right. Little Billy had done me proud.

WOGAN, OR, DISASTER AVERTED

I was due to appear on *Wogan*, the early evening TV chat show, and I planned my movements carefully. I had booked into a hotel so I would not be rushed, and from there I was picked up by car and driven to the studio. I had my own dressing room and the BBC took me up there in plenty of time.

There was no Little Billy for this performance, but I got my uniform and everything I would need out of the bag and hung it up neatly. Then, still with lots of time in hand, I began to change. I put the nice clean shirt on. Tied the tie. Pulled on the uniform trousers with the nice sharp creases. My shoes were over by my bag on the floor. I fetched them, sat on a stool and prepared to put them on. Then it hit me. I was wearing pink socks.

Oh, my goodness, what was I going to do? I just knew that one of my colleagues would spot them if I wore them on television. What on earth *could* I do? There was no time to send out for a new pair of proper black socks. I was stuck, wasn't I?

With me that day was a publicity girl from the BBC, called Laura. She was wearing trousers. With gathering interest I looked down at her ankles. Navy blue. She was wearing navy blue somethings. But what? Don't say tights, I prayed, as I gathered my courage and asked her.

They were pop-socks, she confessed. Bless her. *And* she was willing to help. A big sigh of relief from me, a couple of quick tugs from Laura, and the socks were handed over. I pulled them on top of my pink ones, and was saved. In the studio no one noticed a pair of slightly bulging navy-blue ankles; nor did anyone who saw the programme, so far as I know. In fact, the episode of the pink socks has remained a secret known to very few . . . until today.

It is amazing, though, isn't it, the things you find yourself worrying about when you know that you are in the public eye and that others will be watching and ready to criticize. In an ordinary day's work I may have to go down a 300-foot cliff on a rope, or try and corner an ill-tempered bull, and not think anything of it. But threaten me with being seen on television wearing pink socks instead of dark ones – and I'm terrified. That's show business, I suppose.

–Landy, Our Champion–

Orlando was six last April. He is our marmalade cat and we call him Landy for short. He has become a Double Supreme Premier champion cat of the Cat Association of Great Britain, and part of our sitting-room is filled from floor to ceiling with rosettes that he has won. He is a well-muscled animal, fit and handsome; not at all like the scrawny kitten he was when I first came across him.

I was patrolling a farming area where there had been a lot of flooding. One of the things I was concerned about was seeing that all the sheep had been taken up to higher ground. Somewhere along the road I made a routine stop, like many others I had made that day, and got out of my van to have a general look round.

As I stood there, a strange sound came to my ears. It was like the sound of someone crying. I listened. It wasn't quite a human cry, and I could tell that it was coming from more than one voice. I walked back along the road towards the sound. In a ditch beside the road I saw a cardboard box. I pulled it out of the ditch and placed it on the grass verge, then opened the flaps on top of the box and looked inside.

Four very young kittens lay on the floor of the box; wet through, very cold, stiff, probably close to death. They had obviously been in the ditch for a long time, and my first priority was to warm them up and try and put a bit more life into them. I carried them to my van and got the heater going. I gave each kitten a rub-down to dry them off and stimulate their circulation, then I put them in a basket on the floor of the van, turned up the blower as far as it would go and drove off to Leeds Animal Home. There I took the kittens up to the Cattery on the first floor and put them safely into care.

Of the four kittens in the litter, three were males and one a female. The males were all ginger tabbies and the female was a grey striped tabby, probably like her mother. At first very slowly, then more steadily the kittens recovered, and began to grow and gain strength.

Landy was the runt of the litter, a little pile of rags infested with fleas; at times we wondered about his future. All he seemed to do in his time at the Animal Home was to refuse to die. Still, we found him a home to go to just as we found homes for the other three and soon the time approached when the cardboard-box kittens would be ready to leave and each make a fresh start in a home where it would be wanted and cared for. Then we had a setback.

The woman who had agreed to take Landy fell seriously ill. She was taken into hospital and shortly died. While the other kittens were all assured of their next home, we had to start again with Landy. This time, however, no one was interested in him. To be frank, he didn't look up to much, so it wasn't altogether surprising. Eventually the time came when we had to think very seriously about him. If there were no takers for him, he could not stay indefinitely at the Cattery; he would have to be put down.

By then the other three had gone. Left by himself, Landy looked even more forlorn and pathetic than he had when he was surrounded by his two brothers and sister. I also noticed that, when the subject of Landy was raised at the Cattery, the staff were beginning to look at me in a rather direct way. Although nobody said anything, I had the feeling that I was being politely and quietly leaned on. 'What's going to happen to him, then?' someone would say of the kitten. Then all eyes turned to me.

I thought about it. So far as I could see, it didn't entirely make sense. Just because I had happened to rescue this particular little orange bundle from almost certain death in a ditch, did that really mean I wanted to take him home with me and make him my pet cat? Our pet cat, rather, because my wife Sue would have to share in the decision.

I thought about it some more. If every stray or mistreated animal that I dealt with in the course of my work was to end up living in my house, I would need a castle and several dozen acres to keep them all in. By that line of thinking, I could not really feel guilty or blame myself if I said: no, I'm very sorry, enough is enough, we will have to let him go.

On the other hand – why does there always have to be another hand? – it was true that we did not at that time have either a cat or a dog in the house. We could, therefore, take in this hapless runt without any fear of upsetting a resident animal – who would probably have eaten him in the first five minutes. I decided to take the problem home to Sue.

I am not sure if she was keen or not, but she said she would like to look at him first before she made up her mind. We drove down to the Animal Home, went upstairs to the Cattery and there he was. Sue picked him up and inspected him. There wasn't much to see, but she must have seen something she liked because it didn't take her long to decide. Her answer was yes. We took him home, and from that day we had a cat in our family.

He continued to be a ball of nothing for the first few days, and then he began to respond to his treatment – a lot of careful feeding, grooming and affection supplied by Sue – and to take an interest in life. He started to bounce, like any ordinary kitten does, and to develop his own distinctive character, which we liked. In this way, with our help, he got himself off the danger list and settled into a normal everyday routine.

I have said that we did not have any other cats or dogs in the house and that is true. We did, however, have Shirley and Laverne. They were two rats which Sue had adopted from the Animal Home. As happened with Landy, Sue had not gone looking for these rats. Some animals, somehow, have a way of finding us, and Shirley and Laverne had settled in happily.

Anyone who has kept a rat as a pet will know that they do not live very long, about three years on average, which is a pity because that does not give you much time with them. When Landy came to live with us, Shirley and Laverne were reaching the end of their days, and in due course they died. Then, once more out of the blue, the Animal Home had two more rats needing homes. By now we had a bit of a name as the local rat experts so we were asked if we could have these next two as well. We said yes, and they were soon installed.

The new rats were called Norah Rattie and Rosie, and they became great friends with Landy, especially Norah. After a while Rosie died, and Landy and Norah developed a wonderful rapport, far beyond anything you would normally expect to see between a cat and a rat, traditionally two of Nature's biggest enemies. Their life together is a story by itself, and one day I hope to get round to telling it in detail.

Landy was eighteen months old when Sue and I decided to go down to London to see the National Cat Show at Olympia. This is one of the biggest cat shows in the world, and Sue thought it would be nice if we took Landy with us and entered him in the Novice Class.

I wasn't entirely convinced about this. I was happy that Landy would not let himself, or us, down. He was by now a good-looking prosperous cat with a splendid marmalade coat, thanks to Sue's many hours of patient grooming. No, my slight worry was that going to competitions was very time-consuming, the kind of hobby that can take over your life if you aren't careful. Still, I knew that Sue was very keen, so I agreed that we should give it a go, secretly thinking that a fruitless trip to London might at least help to wear down Sue's enthusiasm. A couple of those, I thought, and she might go off the whole thing.

So down to London we went, and exhibited our Orlando, the grown-up version of a wet and emaciated rest home for fleas which I had found in a ditch not all that long ago.

He swept through the field. He took two Firsts and two Highly Commendeds. Not only that, he won so many tins of food, he paid off in one brief afternoon's work all our expenses over the previous seventeen months. He also won some beautiful Waterford Crystal, which his owners were delighted to take charge of on his behalf.

As we travelled back to Leeds that evening, my brain reeled with the implications for the future. A few hours before, I had been co-owner of a nice marmalade cat going to his first show. Now I sat in the company of a very special animal indeed. What was it he had won? Best Ginger Cat, Best Rescued Cat, Highly Commended Novice and Highly Commended Cat Which Had Travelled More Than One Hundred Miles. How about that for a first outing? Yes, and it was unlikely to be his last. Far from stifling Sue's enthusiasm for cat shows, I had seen her and Landy set themselves up in a hobby that would occupy them for years ahead – and bring some dramatic changes to the décor of our sitting-room.

We went to the Merseyside Cat Show and he won there. It was just amazing to watch him because you would have thought he had known about this cat show caper all his life. Nothing seemed to put him off, and quite soon I noticed that he actually enjoyed getting all those rosettes. He would sit by them quite calmly, as if to say to any passer-by: 'You want to know who won that? Well, who do you think it was?'

We don't need to hold him, or keep him steady in any way. If anyone is in charge, he is. He now appears quite regularly on television and he just sits there and lets everyone else, his admirers, do all the work.

The next step in Landy's show career took place when we joined the Cat Association of Great Britain, as founder members. This is a terrific organization which treats all cats the same, moggies and pedigree animals alike. We entered Landy in the Association's cat shows and again he started winning. At the same time he was collecting some tremendous marks from the judges: rows of 'Excellent, Excellent, Excellent' and very few that were less than 'Very Good'.

We entered him for the Championships of the Cat Association of Great Britain. To win through and become a Champion Cat, he had to win championship certificates from three separate judges. He did so, and was then entitled to go in for the Grand Championship. He became a Grand Champion, and after that he became a Supreme Champion. Then he did it again, so now he is a double Supreme Champion.

I was just amazed by the whole thing. From less than nowhere, from his nearly fatal beginnings in a cardboard box this scrawny waif had grown into an opulent cat about which experienced show judges wrote glowing reviews, e.g. 'Difficult to fault this cat. Has all the ingredients to make a loved and lovable household pet. I wouldn't even suggest that he loses any weight.'

In other words, he may have been very slightly overweight, but, judged as a household pet, he was just about perfect. That, in my view, is the best way to judge animals which are, first and foremost, domestic pets. All cats are welcome to take part in the shows run by the Cat Association of Great Britain, and all have a chance of winning a contest where it is not breed standards which count but the general appearance, fitness and health of the entrants. It doesn't matter if the cat's father was the tom next door, rather than some ornately combed princeling with a flowery name. If the cat, any cat, has got what it takes, it too can be a winner. The Cat Association of Great Britain does a tremendous job in promoting the welfare of cats on a nationwide scale, and I am happy to support them when I can.

I know that Landy has got what it takes, because every so often he pulls out something extra special. He did this once at a cat show when he needed just one more champion's certificate to become a Grand Champion.

He had already been before two judges, and they hadn't given him it. He had won first prize, but he hadn't done quite well enough to earn the champion's certificate. Then he was due to appear before the last judge. It was as if he *knew* he had to produce that little bit extra. He played up, he purred, he nuzzled the lady judge; he did it all to such good effect that a few moments later the lady found she couldn't help but give him his certificate. On the strength of that he became a Grand Champion.

It was a very wise performance, but then I am convinced that cats do understand more than we ever give them credit for. They understand our language as well as their own, and just by looking and observing they seem to have that marvellous knack of knowing what is going on, and how and when they should do something about it.

At some stage in Landy's rise to fame in feline circles, I began to see what a good ambassador he could become for an RSPCA inspector out on his rounds. I started taking him with me to schools and to girl guide and brownie evenings. He was ever so good, and everyone loved him. He let children take his collar off and groom him; with him there I was able to demonstrate in a much more effective way how to be a good and responsible pet owner. 'Look,' he could almost say to his audiences, 'I have to have a collar with a name tag on it, so that people can always tell who I am.'

Because he has such a marvellous temperament, children can get in really close and in him they can see the pet that they themselves would like to own one day. His calmness is also a great boon in the television studio. He is now pretty well shock-proof. Bright flashing lights do not throw him; he just sits there. He has become quite a celebrity after his appearances on *Whiskers and Wet Noses*, a Yorkshire TV show about cats and dogs, on the *Children in Need* programme, and in various news items in which he is asked to appear because the producers know how much enjoyment he gives to the viewers.

When you think about it, animals can do a lot for people. Guide dogs, police dogs and horses, dogs for the blind and the deaf – they lead the way as working helpers. But we sometimes forget how much our ordinary pets do to make our lives interesting and to keep us cheerful. Landy has certainly repaid any kindness that we have shown him over the years. He has been a wonderful pet, and he has definitely made my job a lot easier just by being there when I go to speak to a group about animal welfare. In addition, I know he has given pleasure to a lot of other people through his public appearances. In private or in public, he has definitely got what it takes. We would be lost without him.

Witches Beware

The supernatural is never far from the surface of daily life. In Yorkshire there seem to be witches all over the place, though on the whole my encounters with them have been friendly. There are, of course, white witches as well as black ones, and those I hear from tend to be the sort who anxiously ring up after some nasty sacrifice has come to light:

'It wasn't us,' they say. 'We don't do that sort of thing.' Then they slightly damage their peaceful image by adding: 'And if we do get hold of whoever did it – we'll give 'em bloody what for!'

Some aspects of witchcraft, are, nevertheless, distasteful to many people, and there are some unpleasant things in this chapter which you may prefer not to read. If that is so, I suggest you move straightaway to the next chapter.

To begin on a minor note, I am not too worried about curses. I learned early on in my career how to deal with them. In the chapter called 'Jenkins the Goose' I described how a lady in the hills of West Wales put a curse on me, saying: 'You will never smile again.'

Fortunately, my Welsh background had already taught me that you could destroy the power of a verbal curse by putting one back on the person. I did so, and the lady went so white I thought she was going to pass out. Later, I brought a prosecution against her and her companion for causing unnecessary suffering to animals. At the time I wondered if this would somehow reactivate the curse, but as far as I am aware I have kept on smiling without any ill effects.

I was called out, another time, to deal with a cat which had been vilely mistreated. Whoever was responsible had nailed it to a door, crucifying it and causing it terrible injuries from which it had died. Not long after, I received a telephone call. A voice told me that I had interfered with an important ritual and would be made to suffer for it. Whether that was a curse, I was not sure. Anyway, nothing else happened.

The scene of another, most bizarre case was a cemetery. This was, by any standards, a nasty affair, disgusting in its details. As part of a witches' ritual, a dog had been sacrificed. It had been cut up while it was still alive and must have died a gruesome death.

Whoever had done it knew what they were up to, because the body had been carefully dissected and the blood and internal organs removed. Whether they had used the blood for ceremonial purposes I do not know, but they had washed out the body and then assembled the remains on a gravestone in the shape of a five-pointed star. That alone suggests there had been some form of devil worship going on.

We exposed this nauseating piece of violence to the press, but they did not really want to help. Newspaper editors are loath to show pictures of animals that have been killed and their bodies mutilated because they know they will offend many readers. I realize that such material is offensive to most people's tastes, and so it should be, but at times I feel that the public needs a reminder to make them aware of the dreadful things that a minority continue to inflict on animals, often to a household pet which, who knows, might have been sleeping peacefully in its owner's house just a few hours earlier.

It is always difficult to measure the size of such minorities. I was not surprised, when this last story eventually came out on BBC Television, to receive a phone call from a group of witches. As usual, their message revealed the strange double standard that such people operate in order to keep their activities secret. At first they wanted to blame me for meddling in the occult, and they were quite fierce in the way they put this across. I then replied that, as far as I was concerned, they could wear what they liked and dance round in circles to their heart's content, but as soon as they started to inflict cruelty on animals, they could expect to hear from me. Oh, they said, switching immediately to the defensive, *we* don't do that sort of thing, we are never cruel to animals. That wasn't us, we're white witches. We only work to promote good in the world, etc. etc.

Some of these people may be telling the truth; it is hard to decide one way or the other. Their problem is that by being so furtive about their so-called religion, they create extra difficulties for themselves. The general public and the authorities are bound to be suspicious about *all* witches when they hear about graveyard ceremonies and mutilated dogs – even though some witches may be as harmless as a bunch of nudists on Brighton beach.

Meanwhile, the mysteries continue. A month or so later we

were called out to a wood to investigate what we thought was a gang of people involved in badger-baiting, one of those very cruel sports that flourished in the Middle Ages and, though banned, still surfaces from time to time. A woman living nearby had seen something suspicious at night, possibly to do with animals being tied up. We located the spot, and found that a hole had been dug; in it was a large sack. It felt fairly squashy and we opened it with some trepidation, fearing we might have discovered a corpse. Inside was a bundle of cloaks and scarves, indicating that a coven of witches had been using this wood for their secret meetings.

That evening I had taken with me a lady reporter from a local newspaper, and a photographer. After we had found the witches' cloaks, I said to the photographer: 'You just stay here a minute while we go further on to see if we can find anything else.'

I walked on with the reporter. Next thing, we heard footsteps rushing through the wood behind us. It was the photographer; he was terrified.

'No way am I standing back there on my own!' he declared. It had taken no more than thirty seconds for the creepy atmosphere of the place to give him a bad case of the quivers.

Once again, when our evening's work was reported, this time in a local newspaper, a phone call came through from a member of a coven of witches. She wanted us to understand that it was not their coven which met in the wood; they didn't go dancing around in black cloaks. As a gesture of goodwill she even offered to make the lady reporter some special perfume to protect her from evil spirits.

I saw to it that the cloaks were got rid of. Despite this affront to believers in witchcraft and the supernatural, I heard no more about the incident. Nor, unfortunately, did anyone have the kindness to offer *me* a bottle of magic perfume.

FESTER THE PYTHON AND A RAT CALLED PLAGUE

Then there was Morticia. Viewers of *Animal Squad* may remember that she was the young woman who kept a strange, weirdly named menagerie in her house, and herself slept in a coffin upstairs.

The first I heard of this woman was when the headmistress of a comprehensive school called me one evening on our telephone advisory service. She told me that she and the parents of one of her girl pupils were worried about the way this girl had changed from being a decent, likeable person into a morose, moody girl who was becoming a disruptive influence. One day in school, during a Religious Education class, she had told the mistress that she was visiting a witch. In the witch's house she had watched a dog being dissected and the bits put into a freezer.

This was not long after the discovery of the cut-up dog on the gravestone, and I immediately wondered if there was a connection. Next day I spoke to the girl's father who confirmed what the headmistress had told me, adding that his daughter was now wearing a tattoo on her forearm, and another on her stomach, which looked like occult symbols.

From the headmistress I learned the name of the street where the witch lived, and it was then an easy matter to locate the actual house. No one was at home when we made our first call, so I went to the girl's house and spoke to her parents and then to the girl when she came home from school. During this interview the girl denied that she herself had been inside the witch's house, but she seemed to know that a lot of unusual animals lived there. She mentioned a pig, tarantulas and snakes. Her father told her to roll up her right sleeve: on the forearm was a rough, home-made tattoo of a five-pointed star.

Later that evening I was able to intercept the witch as she returned to her house. I explained who I was and that I had come to see about some of the animals she kept. She invited me inside to look at her 'menagerie'.

She was younger than I had expected, perhaps in her early twenties, plump and with long black hair reaching halfway down her back. She seemed unsurprised by my visit, and showed me into a dimly-lit room smelling of joss sticks. Around the walls were tanks and cages containing a very strange collection of animals. In the next few minutes I was introduced to a six-foot python called Little Lurch, and to two baby pythons about three feet long. Their names were Fester and It. I saw two hamsters, five rats – Plague, Pestilence, Destruction, Blog and Bleb – and a large one-eyed rabbit called Cyclops. The woman, who by then had told me that she called herself Morticia, also showed me her two chinchillas, four cats and – a final surprise – a large hairy tarantula which she drew out from a box, held up in the palm of her hand and kissed.

'This is Tish, short for Morticia,' she said, offering it to me to hold.

I admired the giant spider briefly, but then it was time to get down to some serious questioning. The witch did not deny that schoolgirls had been to the house. She explained that a lot of the local kids were curious about her activities and sometimes were a nuisance, stealing from her and yelling 'Witchy woman' at her. Later she denied knowing anything about a girl with a tattoo on her arm in the shape of a five-pointed star. A brass version of the star lay on a nearby table as I asked her; she explained that she was into the occult 'but only in a small way and I wouldn't do anything to hurt anybody'.

I asked her whether she had a feeezer containing a dead animal. She said no, but she *had* carried out an autopsy on a puppy which had been dead for about six hours. The owners had wanted to know what had been wrong with the puppy, so they had asked her to find out.

No, she went on, she was not qualified to carry out an autopsy. On the other hand, as an artist she understood a lot about anatomy and so had been able to do it. To support her artistic claims, there were a few bits and pieces of sculpture in the room. Thus far, she had answered all my questions reasonably, and if she was telling the truth she had committed no offence under the Animal Acts that I try to enforce. All the creatures in her so-called menagerie were well fed and in good condition.

There remained the strange matter of the coffin-bed, and I questioned her about it. She smiled and asked me if I would like to see it.

I followed this plump, black-haired Yorkshire witch up a flight of stairs to a small bedroom. A sign above the dressing-table said 'Leeds City Mortuary'. In the meagre light from a red bulb I saw a hammer, a crystal ball and a print of a strange creature with blood pouring from its mouth. Under the window, on a table, stood a mahogany coffin with brass handles. On the lid of the coffin, a brass plate was inscribed with the words: 'Morticia Crowley/1465 to 1490'.

The 'real' Morticia explained that the coffin had been made

specially for her. She opened the lid and inside were a blanket and pillow, the blanket untidily creased and turned back on one side – just like an unmade bed.

That, barring a few more questions, was the end of it. I had no formal accusation to make. I warned her about letting young children witness disturbing acts with animals and she accepted the warning without demur, although she had previously maintained that the only witness to the dissection of the dog had been one of its owners.

I left the house, reflecting that my first-hand experience of witchcraft had for the most part been fairly harmless, even though none of it was to my personal taste. I also remembered, as I made my way back to the office, that it was Friday the 13th.

—— THE SQUIRREL TRAP ——

By far the majority of people convicted of cruelty to animals are more than twenty-two years old. In the Leeds area we have had only three juvenile court cases in fourteen years.

The case of the squirrel in the wood was one of the exceptions. It was also a case which incensed a lot of people because of the severe cruelty inflicted on the animal. The boy responsible was only sixteen years of age.

I was called with a colleague to a wood. Someone had reported seeing a boy with a squirrel which he had caught. He put it into a kind of home-made pen and threw stones at its head, then he released it, caught it again because it was too dazed to get away, and put it back in the pen and repeated the process.

We made our approach from the edge of the wood. If we were quick enough, we might still catch him at it. Fate then intervened as we climbed a row of spiked railings which ran across our path. In my haste, I mistimed my jump down on the other side and impaled one arm on a spike.

My mishap with the railing was enough to save the boy for the time being. He heard us, stopped what he was doing with the squirrel, and ran off through the wood. There was little hope of catching him but we were able to locate the squirrel. It had a definite bump on its head and was obviously in a very dazed condition. We put it in a basket and placed this in the back of my van to take it to the Animal Home for veterinary treatment. I was also looking forward to having my arm treated, because the spike had left me with a nasty injury. (What made me even more annoyed was that when we gave up the chase and went back to find the squirrel, I saw a woman, out exercising her dog; she walked up to those same railings, lifted out a loose one and slid herself through with no trouble at all!)

We set off for the Animal Home and then, quite by chance, as we were driving down a nearby road, we spotted the boy again. We stopped the van sharply, jumped out and nabbed him before he had a chance to escape, and took him straight down to the police station.

He was held there while his parents were contacted and later we interviewed him in the presence of his mother. If he felt any shame for what he had done, he was at great pains to keep it hidden. Towards us he was truculent, indifferent. He couldn't care less – at least, that was his message to us. After I had cautioned him, I managed with some difficulty to take a statement from him and then I warned him that I would be reporting him for causing unnecessary suffering to an animal, and that he would be prosecuted.

I made my recommendations to Headquarters, and at this point we came up against what to me are some strange loopholes in the law. First of all, can you be cruel to a squirrel? As far as I was concerned, a squirrel, even though it is a wild animal, should be entitled to the same protection that is given to a cat, or a dog or a farm animal. Recent cases, however, had shown that not all animals were equal in the eyes of the law; in one case, in which the victim was a hedgehog, the magistrates had decided that there was no charge to answer. In other words, you cannot be cruel to a hedgehog.

Our lawyers also said we would have to prove that the squirrel was a captive animal. A statement in the Divisional Court had said that with a wild animal captivity had to mean that it was held on more than a temporary basis, and that a period of time had to elapse during which 'acts of dominion' were exercised over it. If the squirrel could not be said to have been in a state of captivity, we would not be able to bring the prosecution.

What the boy had in fact done was to build a four-sided container from loose bricks, in which he placed the squirrel when he had caught it. To prevent it from escaping, he had got a piece of wood which he laid over the top. We were able to establish that the boy had built the container *before* he caught the squirrel. He must therefore have been confident that he *would* be able to catch it; this made us think that he had been indulging in this home-made and very unpleasant type of squirrel-baiting on previous occasions.

However, we still had to satisfy the legal requirement that the squirrel was held in a state of captivity, and that the boy had 'dominion' over it. My own feelings were that the law was asking too much. I believe that you *can* be cruel to a hedgehog, and, what is more, I also believe that you do not have to hold a wild animal prisoner in order to be cruel to it. If a squirrel was up a tree and someone threw bricks at it, that would be cruelty as I understand the meaning of the word. That is my view; but then I do not write the laws of the land.

We were also questioned very closely about the squirrel's injuries and whether the boy had really been responsible for them. My colleague and I had both seen the boy throwing stones at the squirrel when we first tried to catch him, so there was no doubt in our minds that he was responsible. Yes, said our advisers, but had he been responsible for *all* the squirrel's injuries? It might well be that we would have to prove this to the court.

I explained how I saw it. This boy had built a receptacle out of bricks and placed a piece of wood over the top to confine the squirrel. After hitting it with a stone and prodding it with a stick, he released it in an exhausted condition. He then threw further stones at it, by which time the animal was in severe shock and unable to move. When I arrived on the scene with my colleague, and the boy dashed off, we had no difficulty in taking the squirrel into care. In the intervening minutes it had managed to get as far as a tree but it was so exhausted that I had only to reach out and take hold of it.

As for the severity of the squirrel's injuries, in my view there was no doubt that the animal showed obvious signs of illness and external injury. It was dazed and unco-ordinated in its movements and it had a bump on its head. The vet backed us up, saying that it was in a state of real shock when he examined it. Further proof of the severity of the injuries came five days after the incident, when the squirrel died. A post-mortem was carried out and this showed that it had suffered damage to the brain.

On these grounds, we went ahead with our prosecution and it was successful. I was able to prove to the magistrates that the boy, who admitted throwing a stone at the squirrel, had maimed the animal and made it incapable of escaping, so that it was in effect in a state of captivity. The magistrates also accepted as further proof the ease with which I had picked up the squirrel and placed it in my basket; it must have been dazed and shocked to have allowed me to do this without resisting.

The boy was found guilty and fined, and ordered to pay the fine out of his own pocket. I had hoped that the experience of being taken to court would have made him somewhat sorry for what he had done – sorrier, at least, than he was when I first questioned him. But he gave no sign of a change of heart, and when the chairman of the bench asked him if he had anything to say, his answer was a very blunt: 'Nowt'.

The chairman, however, told him that he regarded what he had done as a serious offence and he should at least give an assurance that he would not do it again. He then imposed the fine and the case was closed.

It had taken us a lot of time and effort to bring this particular prosecution but to my mind it had been very worthwhile. It was not inconceivable that the boy had been affected by what he had been put through, and we could therefore hope that in time he would learn to control his more savage instincts and take a more responsible attitude. In the meantime, we had successfully defended the principle that an animal – even a wild animal such as a squirrel – is entitled at all times to protection from cruelty. The success of this case would make it easier for other similar cases to be brought in the future, we hoped.

— Widely Different — — Callings —

It is amazing how in my work I can become drawn into other people's lives. The involvement may begin with taking an old man's dog down to the vet for him; it may end with taking charge of the same man's funeral.

That was about the weight of it with old Mr Caley, plus a few extra complications. No matter what they tell you at the RSPCA training school about the work being varied, and your needing to be tactful and on your toes all the time, until you experience it you can't really be sure what they are on about. 'Your work combines many widely different callings,' they say. 'At times you need to be a lawyer, a veterinary surgeon, an organizer of other people.' No mention, you will notice, of being a home help, a stand-up comedian or a funeral director. They leave you to find out those bits for yourself.

It was a lady on the local RSPCA branch committee who introduced me to Mr Caley. He had been ill and unable to take his dog to the vet for treatment; could I help by taking the dog down there for him? I said I would be only too pleased.

The dog soon recovered, but Mr Caley did not. Soon I was going along to his flat to take the dog out for regular walks; then I was doing a bit of shopping for the old feller, and caring for him as well. In a way it was only natural; he lived alone in a flat on a council estate, and although he had relatives nearby, none of them wanted the bother of looking after him and his dog.

Mr Caley's condition grew worse. He had cancer and was now very ill. He was losing strength as well as weight, but he refused to go into hospital; partly, I am sure, this was because he did not want to face being parted from his dog. When I went to the flat I was having to do more and more for him – even carrying him to the toilet, after which I had to clean and wash him as well.

At last, one day, after much putting-off and silent contemplation of our assurances that his dog would be well looked after, he agreed to be admitted to hospital. The ambulance came to fetch him and take him in, and I looked forward to visiting him in a hospital ward instead of calling at the flat. At least, I thought to myself, I won't have to carry him to the toilet any more. That was a little presumptuous of me.

On arrival at the hospital for my first visit, I was summoned into the Sister's office. Sister seemed rather embarrassed, apologetic.

'Mr Caley has been waiting for you to arrive so he can go to the toilet,' she told me at last.

I then heard how Mr Caley had first of all said no to a bedpan, following that up with: 'No female is going to see me without my clothes on!' He and the hospital staff faced an awkward future, I thought, unless I was prepared to co-operate.

'All right,' I said, 'just this once.' I went in to see him.

Later, as we struggled back from the toilet, I tried to persuade him to let a nurse look after him the next time the need arose. 'It's not personal,' I said. 'This is a hospital, they've seen it all before.'

I was not sure if I had won him over, but he soon fell into the hospital way of life. The drugs he was taking no doubt played a part. These, added to the exhaustion brought on by his illness, made him too weak to offer lasting resistance.

He settled in at the hospital and it did him some good. He noticed this change in himself and began to speak of the day when he might return to his flat and be reunited with his beloved dog. However, it was not to be. One afternoon I received a radio call to contact the hospital, and they told me that my friend had passed peacefully away. He had fought the disease bravely and without complaint.

I thanked them. It seemed that my association with Mr Caley was almost over. All I had to do was find a good home for the dog – who meanwhile had been staying in kennels – and that would be the end of the matter. I was wrong. Even in death this old feller was not letting us go.

A couple of days later I received some startling news. The lady committee member told me over the telephone that Mr Caley had named us as next-of-kin, and therefore we now had the responsibility of arranging his burial. We made further inquiries and found that there were no assets remaining beyond a couple of pounds from his pension, plus £30 from the death grant.

The authorities suggested a pauper's grave. For reasons I cannot quite explain, I felt this was an unworthy solution. During the eighteen months I had known old Mr Caley I had learned much about him. He had been proud to have fought for his country and had often shown me his service medals and talked about his exploits. Perhaps it was this pride, and also the fact that he had become more than just a casual or 'business' acquaintance, that made me refuse to accept that he should be finally rewarded with the grave of a pauper.

From a funeral director we learned that we would need a further £200 to give the old feller the send-off he deserved. I was determined that we must somehow raise the money; but how?

I knew that Mr Caley had once belonged to a club where I was still a member. I contacted the club secretary and he agreed to help. As a result I spent several evenings working at the club as an entertainer. I told jokes and threw in some magic tricks in an effort to meet the funeral expenses. I had told the undertaker how I intended to raise the money to pay for the funeral and he had agreed to go ahead and make his arrangements, saying that he would wait for the money until I had got it all together.

He did not have long to wait. My earlier appearances had earned a certain amount for our funeral fund but we still had a good way to go when the club secretary came up with a new idea. He told me he could get two sections of the club to sponsor me for £50 each provided I could tell jokes non-stop for an hour, and did not repeat a joke. I accepted, groaning inwardly, and so, one evening a few days later, launched into the longest hour of my life.

If you are thinking of trying it yourself, I can at least say this: take your time. Speak slowly so that you make each joke last as long as possible, and, if the audience is gracious enough to laugh, use every scrap of their laughter to eke out your performance.

After what seemed like two and a half months of this, I was in the middle of a joke when the audience started clapping. Not because I was being funny but because the hour was up. I was exhausted. However, I perked up when they handed over the winnings.

Old Mr Caley got his decent funeral in the end – all bought and paid for. There can't be many people who have been buried by the RSPCA, and it is sad that we had to take on the role of being a substitute family. I am not intending to make a habit of it.

TINKERING WITH NATURE

In an earlier chapter, 'Crufts and Ruffs', I looked at the way some pedigree dog breeders allow themselves to be swayed by financial considerations, particularly in the way they treat their animals at home and prepare them for lucrative dog shows. There is more to be said on this subject, which involves two basically distinct but overlapping topics, those of breeding techniques and cosmetic surgery.

It worries me that Man is expecting too much of pedigree dogs. There is now a lot of evidence of overbreeding, the process by which owners and breeders seek to extend characteristics in their animals which I am sure the dogs would never have developed by themselves if Nature had been left to take its course.

This urge, which is driven by commercial considerations, shows itself in a number of ways. Some alterations are brought about by breeding techniques. At their worst these produce animals which are so over-refined that the poor creatures cannot function properly as dogs: Bulldogs who can't breathe efficiently because of the bred-in damage to their noses, or Bloodhounds who have trouble eating because their over-large jowls get in the way. Some of these practices have now reached a stage where the future of entire breeds is being put at risk. As ever, I suspect that money is doing the talking, at the expense of common sense.

Over-breeding can also affect a dog's mentality. You get the Rage Syndrome, for instance: this occurs when certain types of dog become over-protective towards a possession or trophy – a bone or a piece of blanket which they decide is theirs and no one else is allowed near it. Whether this tendency was present in the original dog we do not know, but it is the kind of defect which over-breeding is more than likely to aggravate and make more common.

Let's now consider some of the common instances of cosmetic surgery, and first of all what is meant by the term. As I understand it, cosmetic surgery is the principal means used by owners and breeders to satisfy their own, i.e. selfish, desires to change the appearance of an animal, to make it more 'beautiful' in their eyes.

One practice I particularly dislike is tail docking. It is quite unnecessary, and to my mind cruel, to remove something which is part of an animal's natural physical state. If God had not meant dogs to have tails, He wouldn't have given them one. Dogs use their tails for signalling and as an aid to balance, and it must be wrong to deprive them of these faculties or to force them to make do with a silly little stump.

All right, it would take a bit of time to get used to seeing Cocker Spaniels with long bushy tails, but if enough owners were to speak up now and say: no more docked tails, then full-length tails would soon enough become standard for all the breeds concerned.

I accept fully that there are times when it is necessary for medical reasons to dock a tail or remove a claw, even to de-bark a dog or crop an ear. But to do this simply to make an animal look 'pretty' or acceptable at a show is, to my mind, disgusting.

Dogs are the most common victims of cosmetic practices, but there is one that applies particularly to cats. This is the dreadful business of de-clawing. To remove a cat's claws for no better reason than because it has been scratching the furniture is not only inexcusable, it also shows that the owner has very little idea of the true nature of his or her pet. A cat without claws becomes a changed animal. Claws are *the* major item in a cat's defensive equipment. Without these highly efficient retractable weapons it has only its teeth to rely on, and these are not nearly as efficient.

Claws are also essential to a cat for moving about, for springing and jumping on to places like walls and tree branches, and getting down from them. If a cat suddenly discovers that it has lost its natural ability to climb and cling on, it will become confused and dejected. Its natural instinct for self-preservation will tell it not to take so many chances and it will very likely respond to that instinct, becoming nervous, unadventurous, withdrawn, a very different animal from what it was before Man came along and ruined it.

I am glad to say that the Royal College of Veterinary Surgeons now disapproves of cosmetic surgery, and I would ask that anyone hearing of a vet willing to de-claw an animal should report him or her to the Royal College. I know that this practice continues, and this is one of those areas where an informed and determined public effort can help a great deal to outlaw something which they feel is unacceptable.

I am also against ear cropping unless there is a good medical reason. Unfortunately, most ear cropping is done to satisfy an owner's desire to make his dog more acceptable to show judges or to make it more appealing when it is taken out for a walk. I do not see how either reason can be justified.

Try looking at it from the dog's point of view, or, at least, let's see what this operation involves and precisely what it sets out to achieve. Say an owner thinks his Dobermann should look more alert than it does. He decides that the answer is to make its ears prick up more. He takes it to the vet and there, under anaesthetic, the gristle at the base of the dog's ears is cut and then stitched in a new position slightly further back on the head so that the ears are pulled backwards and upwards. Result: the dog is still the same dog, as alert or unalert as it ever was, but now it has been cut about to satisfy some quite arbitrary human desire that it should *look* more like an ideal Dobermann.

Ear cropping is now more prevalent in the United States than in Britain, but it does happen here as well. There is also an 'opposite' treatment, to make a lop-eared dog look even more lop-eared (and therefore, so the thinking goes, more friendly and appealing). To achieve this effect, the gristle is cut away so that the ear is in fact more detached from the head than it originally was. To me this is an abuse of the surgeon's art, and should not be allowed except in order to deal with a genuine malformation.

The less serious end of the cosmetic trade is the poodle parlour, where pampered dogs are delivered by adoring owners for a shampoo and set, a trim or a clip or I don't know what. I have nothing against owners doing something that helps to keep their pet clean and well-groomed, but even here more thought could be given to the animal's feelings.

The trouble is, we don't know what they feel. However, they must feel slightly different or strange, I would have thought. Is it too unreasonable to wonder if there is some connection between how I would feel if all my hair (if I had any!) was suddenly shaved in unaccustomed places and the top part scraped and gelled into a funny sort of peak, and how a poodle feels after a 'Lion clip', when its rear end is shaved, leaving only a daft bobble of fur on the end of its tail and other 'bracelets' round its lower legs. Would I feel good about having a poodle parlour hairdo? Probably not. Well then, why should a dog enjoy a similar, even draughtier experience, particularly when it is not being done for his benefit but to satisfy some romantic urge on the part of his owner.

As Eric Morecambe used to say: 'There's no answer to that!'

YORKSHIRE POEMS —— —— FOR PETS ——

As I go about in the course of my work, I am delighted when people tell me about their pets. Some write me letters and recount stories, others send me poems, and lots of schoolchildren send me beautiful paintings. I never cease to wonder at the bonds that unite pets and their owners; how strong they are and long-lasting, continuing even after the pet has passed away.

Here are some samples of our Yorkshire poets at work. My sincere thanks to them all.

MY RABBITS

At home I have some animals
Who have some funny habits,
No, they're not unusual,
Just male and female rabbits.

Every time I feed them
You'd think they were quite starving,
They eat me out of house and home,
Their diet's quite alarming.

They love a good variety,
Creamed spuds and apple flan,
They also like fresh strawberries
Mixed in with their bran.

My 'Dutchess' is a big girl
Especially round the hips,
This will be of no surprise
When I tell you she likes CHIPS!

Lynn Cotton

FANG

I'm a very imperious Cat
Half Chinchilla, half Persian and fat.
Commanding the best easy chair
To disturb me, why, no one would dare.
I've adopted my own special humans.
Well, they feed me and make me their pet
And I choose a warm spot by the fireside
When outdoors it's cold and it's wet.
In appearance I'm handsome and fluffy
My tail seems to float in the breeze
I can lay on my back by the lawn
As I purr and I yawn and I sneeze.
Oh there's no doubt I'm sophisticated
Well, I'm really an aristo-cat.
And I think I'm purrfectly lovely
So who is to argue with that.
I sit up with my paws on the table
I rattle the doors with a bang
Oh, yes, when I'm about then let others look out.
Here comes 'supa puss', here comes FANG.

Elizabeth Smithson, Leeds.

WHAT HAVE I DONE?

Written after seeing the RSPCA programme on the TV about the cruelty to a
dog whose eyes still haunt me with their questioning.

What have I done to deserve such fate?
Pleading eyes beg an answer.
What have I done, that your cold heart
Could find no love, my Master?
I offered you companionship,
And faithfulness till death.
And all I sought was a bite to eat.
A warm place by your Hearth.

Instead I found but cruel kicks.
Rough words instead of kindness.
Hunger. Neglect. My trust you spurned.
How can humans be so mindless?
Now all I seek is oblivion,
A bitter victory you have won.
But I still would like the answer to,
Master, what have I done?

Joyce Everill

THE WILD ONES

They streak across two busy city roads,
With agile feline leaps, high walls to scale,
Appearing on my snow-encrusted fence,
Less wary now the arctic winds prevail.
For hungry kittens make uneasy truce,
With human kind whose love they've never known,
Two saucers filled with tasty food are placed,
Beneath the igloo bush they've made their own,
In no time they are gone – their platters clean.
A trail of paw marks in the virgin snow,
A tracking back to walls and busy roads,
From whence they came – or hide – I'll never know.

Francis Cox, Wakefield.

BEAU

Neglected and unwanted, you didn't know how to play,
They said they didn't want you, so, I took you away,
I gave you love and tenderness, you crept into my heart,
You gave me so much in return, with you I could not part,
You'd follow me around the house, you'd lie there at my feet.
At night you lay upon my bed as I dropped off to sleep,
Your little whimpers wakened me at the start of every day,
I'd stroke your head, and whisper, my pet, you're here to stay.
How you used to welcome me when I'd been out a while,
Your little tail would wag away, I'd look at you and smile,

As years passed on I wouldn't see that you were growing old,
To me you were my little pet and worth your weight in gold,
I prayed you'd never leave me, that wish was not to be,
I never knew how suddenly you'd be snatched away from me,
That day I held you tenderly, I gently stroked your head,
Your tired body's resting now, no more will you feel pain,
And I'd give so much to hold you, in my empty arms again.
So sleep in peace my little pet, I say thanks to God above,
For all the years I had you here, to care for and to love.

Mrs W. Kay, Morley, near Leeds.

THE TROUBLE WITH
ZOOS

One of my greatest ambitions is to go to somewhere like Kenya and see, in the wild, some of the larger animals that up till now I have never encountered face to face except within the confines of a zoo or circus. In the great Nature Reserves these magnificent creatures are free to chase and run with the wind; there are no walls to hold them in and stifle their spirit. They are free to live as Nature equipped them to live.

In recent years, since returning to Yorkshire from Wales, I have had plenty of opportunity to get to know the internal workings of zoos and similar places, and to consider just what I feel is wrong with them. It has not all been a negative experience. In the course of my work, investigating the affairs of Knaresborough Zoo, near Harrogate, where things were going wrong, I came to know and respect a community of, to me, new animals. In particular I admired the larger animals living there, and possibly my favourites were the big cats.

I knew them all by name – Tank the tiger, Kaffa the black leopard, Roma the Sumatran tigress, and many others. I learned about their little idiosyncrasies and got to know the various party tricks which, perhaps through boredom, they had learned to do, like Dandy-Leo the lioness who was locally famous for rolling over on request.

To me it is wrong that such animals should be kept in cages. On the other hand, to see them up close and to be able to form even a slight relationship with them, was very rewarding. It seems contradictory, I know, but the complications arise not from my own feelings but because zoos exist and we have to look after the welfare of the animals as best we can. When I see an animal like a tiger in a wildlife documentary on television, there is no doubt in my mind that I would rather see him at liberty in his natural environment than pacing between the four walls of a cage.

However, while it may be desirable to close down zoos and wildlife parks and not replace them, our first priority is to look after the animals which inhabit them. Most were born in captivity and would have no chance of fending for themselves if they were released in the wild. Many have already reached an age, or state of infirmity, which they very well might not have reached had they been forced to suffer the rough justice of life in the bush. But that is no reason to say, as some do: 'Right. They can't stay here any longer. There's no room for them anywhere else. We'll have to put them down.'

That to me is not what life is about. Life is for living, and we do not have the right simply to take life away when it suits us. Animals in zoos can all too easily become the innocent victims of their surroundings. Their plight is not unlike that of the cat or dog which is given a home and then suddenly is turned out on the street. The essential difference between a household pet and a zoo animal is that you cannot turn a lion or a bear out on the street. The alternatives are: you either find it another home, or you have it put down.

At Knaresborough Zoo, we faced this problem about three hundred times over. The owners of the zoo had fallen on financial hard times; they had been unable to maintain their premises at an adequate level and in due course their annual licence application was refused. The case went to appeal but the owners lost and were then given six months to dispose of their animals and close the zoo.

This all came about because of a comparatively new law, the Zoo Licensing Act of 1981 which came into effect in 1984. The Act is designed to ensure that dangerous animals are properly housed and that the public are protected from them for reasons of both health and safety. Before the Act, the law's coverage of zoos and wildlife parks was fairly haphazard; there was no government department responsible for overseeing the way they were run. It was important that a code of standards was set up and enforced, and this has been done. Now all zoos and similar places have to be licensed, and each year they have to apply for the licence to be renewed.

When it became clear that Knaresborough Zoo would have to close, we had a lot of pressure from people demanding that all zoos should be shut and that in future animals should not be kept in captivity. This was all very well, but when a zoo goes out of business, what happens to the animals?

The simple answer is that if you have ever been close to any of these animals, whether it be a lion, a tiger, a bear or one of the many inhabitants of the reptile house, you do your very best to see them spared and given the chance of a new life elsewhere. At Knaresborough we had to try and do this for the best part of three hundred animals: not the easiest of tasks when you are under the sword of a deadline imposed by the courts, and, what is more, the owner of the zoo is so upset that half the time he can't bring himself to face the reality of what has happened.

We took on the challenge, and in the end I am happy to say that we found homes for all but four of the mammals, birds, fish and reptiles living at the stricken zoo. We coped with all kinds of unforeseen extra problems, as when the local electricity board sent officials to cut off the supply because their bills had not been paid. Of course, as soon as the switch was thrown, all the lights went out and, more important still, all the heaters in the reptile house began to cool. If the heat was not restored in twelve hours, the consequences could be fatal. After a furious round of telephone calls from my end, the electricity board agreed to restore the power supply within one hour of a request for reconnection being made – provided someone also gave an undertaking to pay for the future cost of electricity. RSPCA headquarters responded quickly and generously, agreeing to be responsible for future supplies until the immediate fate of all the animals had been sorted out. So that was one reprieve.

Via BBC Television News, who had a camera crew preparing one news bulletin after another as their story developed, I gave an interview and explained that the RSPCA was trying to find new homes for the animals. The particular point of this message was to do something for the zoo's collection of domestic animals, the goats, cats and rabbits which did not need special living quarters and could perfectly well be taken into private homes. The response from the viewers was immediate. People rang the zoo and the RSPCA and in half an hour all the domestic animals had been found new homes. For me it was a valuable demonstration of television's power to attract instant public interest on a massive scale, and the right sort of responsible interest, too; in the days that followed, now that Knaresborough Zoo was truly on the news map, we heard from a few hopeless optimists and the odd nutter, but in the main we were contacted by people genuinely offering realistic help.

Most of the animals were taken in by other zoos. That was not surprising in that they had the best facilities for absorbing particular groups of animals as well as individuals – the venomous snakes, for instance, or a family of tree bears. Provided these other zoos were licensed, and had adequate accommodation, I felt it was right that the Knaresborough animals should go to them. I was surprised by the criticism we received at the time, but some animal campaigners are perhaps too idealistic: they allow their dislike of zoos to override their concern about the actual welfare of animals that might have nowhere else to go. It was, and is, our policy first and foremost to save an animal if we possibly can.

In the longer term, perhaps we should be looking for a way to limit the numbers of animals being brought into zoos. Perhaps it is time to say: no more imported animals if their fate is to end up in a zoo, a wildlife park or a circus. Certainly I think we could try and put a stop to animals being bred in zoos. It must be true that an animal that has never experienced the wild cannot fully share all the characteristics of its cousin who spends its days roaming freely in the bush, seeking its own food each day, caring for and protecting its family and dealing with its enemies.

Of the animals we saved, some were a good deal luckier than others to find another home. I was particularly pleased for Satan, a very very old lion. At one time I thought he had no chance. Then a plan was put forward to build a den for him at another zoo – provided money could be found to build the den. As soon as news of this was made public, through television, we had a load of donations and work on the den began almost immediately. Satan was transferred to his new home and I hear that he has settled in there very happily.

Another story with a happy ending concerned Roma, the Sumatran tigress. She was getting on in years and no one gave her much of a future. I explained her plight on television and someone contacted the owners of Linton Zoo, near Cambridge, who replied that they had plenty of ground space but lacked an enclosure that was either big enough or built to the safety levels necessary for an animal such as Roma. However, if money could be raised to build an enclosure and sleeping quarters, they were prepared to take her on.

A rescue fund was set up, and while it was still in its early days an RAF sergeant from the Tigers persuaded his mates to make Roma the squadron mascot. 'Tigers' is the nickname for 74 Squadron RAF, which was based not far from Cambridge at Stowmarket, in Suffolk. Their share in the rescue was to offer to pay for Roma's keep for the rest of her life. Other donations were received by BBC Radio Cambridge, and enough money was raised not only to guarantee Roma's future but also to provide a home at the same zoo for Kaffa the black leopard.

Roma is now housed in a brand-new enclosure which is a lot larger than the one she had at Knaresborough. She has put on weight and is in first-class condition. To me that more than justifies the venture. If she is now better off than she was, enjoying better food and better facilities, then I feel that our efforts allowed her to progress in her life, rather than the reverse as some of our critics believe.

My great regret is that in such circumstances the animals are always the victims. Their fates are chosen for them. It is just one of the many unfortunate aspects of zoos and the way they are organized. I hope this can all be changed. Looking to the future, and the possibilities of quicker and cheaper air travel, I hope that one day many more of us living in Britain will be able to make at least one journey to see those animals we admire most in their natural settings. When that begins to happen, the days of the zoo must be numbered.